D1625200

WAYLAND · FREE · PUBLIC · LIBRARY
FOUNDED 1848
INCORPORATED
WAYLAND
1835

B. B. C. E. LIBRARY
950 Metropolitan Ave.
Boston, MA 02136
(617) 364-

Our Best Years

Our Best Years

Helen Hayes
with
Marion Glasserow Gladney

B. C. E. LIBRARY
Metropolitan
Boston, MA 02
(617) 364-3510

Doubleday & Company, Inc.
Garden City, New York
1984

Be T
6.56
9.84

305.26
Hay

Library of Congress Cataloging in Publication Data

Hayes, Helen, 1900–
   Our best years.   ✓ 1. Elderly - U.S.

   1. Aged—United States—Addresses, essays, lectures. 2. Aged—Conduct of life—Addresses, essays,
lectures. I. Gladney, Marion Glasserow. II. Title.
HQ1064.U5 H34   1984   305.2'6   83–25443
ISBN: 0-385-19407-2

Copyright © 1984 by Helen Hayes and
Marion Glasserow Gladney

All Rights Reserved
Printed in the United States of America
First Edition

Acknowledgment

My gratitude to V. J. Skutt, Mutual of Omaha, for his courage to air public affairs commentaries, which erode resistance to "senior" programming.

And a blessing on my Graddy Hayes. She was a comfort and a strength, a lap to fall into and sob when some childhood setback had occurred. She made me aware of the value of the older family members in the home. She taught me to love.

Contents

Introduction

This book was written not with a word processor, but with a friend. It's more fun that way. Although Marion Gladney and I have a mother-daughter time span between us, we seem to think in the same channels. What we both do very well is get older; we regard it as an inevitability and approach it with a sense of humor while making absolutely sure that love and work are at the core of our days on earth.

This is a great time of my life, the best in many ways. I can do what I want, when I want, go where I please—as often and as long as I like. I'm accountable to no one and no one need check in with me. The world is my playground, my workroom, my stage, and my responsibility in a small measure, too. I've been given much. I owe a great deal. What I like about the eighties—mine and the century's—is that this decade is so full of change. The best part of it is that the miracle of modern medicine prolongs health and life so that "old" does not have to sound like punishment. What we need now is to have the social sciences catch up with the medicine men. They have yet to learn what to do with all these eager survivors and all those who reach an age beyond their expectations and don't quite know what to do with it.

To that end, we have addressed these essays. We want to beat this small drum to wake up the young to face the inescapable fact of their own very, very long lives. We want to rattle the traditions of middle management, middle income, middle age, and middle-of-the-roaders to help them realize that "tried and true" methods don't add up when the number projections are for fifty-nine million Americans over sixty-five years old forty-six years from now!

I wanted so much to reach out to that audience with whom I had been on affectionate terms since the days of our youth. Way back then I communicated from stages, safely wrapped in a playwright's invention, hiding inside a character he had dreamed into being. I meet some of these unknown friends when I go to public events. "I saw you in *Victoria Regina* when I was on my honeymoon," they tell me, or "I was a freshman at Yale when I saw *What Every Woman Knows.* I fell in love with your Maggie Wylie," or "My mother took me to see *Mrs. McThing*—my first play. Now I have children of my own. I wish I could take them to see that play." So it goes, on and on. We are all a bit craggy of face now and snowcapped (or dyed), but for the moment we are swept back to youth by a shared memory.

I have spent most of my life interpreting the thoughts and the lives of characters of fiction or history. Since I no longer communicate with my public across the proscenium, I have used the airwaves in recent years. Marion and I have been collaborating for over six hundred broadcasts, daily radio programs that are syndicated throughout the land. It's a challenge to pack useful, palatable information succinctly into short scripts. I jump headlong into research, wading through the overweight New York *Times* as Charlie, my husband, used to do—covering every item, even the ads. It is particularly fascinating to see the aged and aging emerge from the shadows, stepping right out onto center stage and declaring themselves a force to be reckoned with.

By now, there is a sizable audience for my daily two-minute broadcasts, and we manage to encourage a fair number of listeners to consider advancing age with pleasure and as a challenge. We are firmly opposed to abdication. New horizons, new ideas, new activities, new points of view; there is life after sixty-five. That's our message. Of course, it's not the same for men and women; even working women always had that "other job" waiting for them at home.

In this book we touch on many things—including work, health, money, love, friendship, fun. I have, like all of us, found that I cannot recreate the past but must live in the present or, better yet, the future.

The real future belongs to the young, as it always has, and rightfully so. They, in turn, can and must recognize the old in order to see themselves and thereby be motivated to work at improving the quality of life for the long living, *now.*

We have, since the beginning of our history, trained ourselves to be independent—as individuals, as a nation. Perhaps it's time to be educated in *interdependence.*

Having helped to overcome the media's automatic rejection of any material geared to the older population, we also felt compelled to change some of the vocabulary. I think the term "retirement," for instance, is much too negative, almost sleep inducing. "Recreatement" sounds much more encouraging for that last and best third of one's life, which can be filled with newness. And in place of "seniors," "elders," or "aged persons," I offer "maturians." It says there's still a bit of fight in us.

We have had stimulation and encouragement from our listeners—young and old—and from Mutual of Omaha, who makes the broadcasts possible, for which we are very grateful. I am especially delighted at this opportunity to reach a new audience of friends and contemporaries whose needs and struggles and worries and joys are really universal: yours, mine, *ours*. My hope is that you, the reader, will find some inspiration, encouragement, and help in these reflections. I make no claims at expertise in every area but can only offer my own insights from lived experiences or observations.

Above all, as I told a reporter once during a newspaper interview, "We older folks need to be constantly goaded, to keep in there . . . The changes demanded by old age are tough enough to accept. Maintaining as much independence as you can makes it easier to yield gracefully to those changes."

Part 1

Most things are easier said than done. Except love.

FEAR OF INVOLVEMENT

How did we become so estranged from each other? We seem to live in a society so complex that we don't know how to relate—and we've stopped trying. If we see a stranger fall, we assume he's drunk, or drugged, and leave him unattended. Or we fear unfounded lawsuits and give the fellow a wide berth. I saw a blind man tapping his way down a city street—right into the down stairwell to the subway. Since it took him by surprise, he fell. People closer to him than I was didn't help him until I rushed over.

We are afraid to *touch:* we fear involvement and responsibility. There was a time when families cared for each other's children, when adults could admonish someone else's child and not fear the wrath of the parents. Now we have turned away from each other, and the results are devastating—staggering. I read that there are as many as twenty thousand runaway children under sixteen years old in New York City. You can find many of them in Times Square—our illustrious theater-district-turned-sewer—selling their bodies in the most unspeakable ways. Boys and girls! The results are broken bodies, disease, murder, rape, drugs.

The ten o'clock newscasters ask us whether we know where our children are. Shouldn't they be inquiring whether we care? It's time to turn off the TV and get involved in the real world.

FATHERS

The mother who was too abashed to acknowledge that the sand-throwing child at the beach was hers called out, "Young man, if you don't stop immediately, I'll tell your father!" Funny, but unfair. I think perhaps today's parents don't participate in this type of divisiveness. If we look back at our own parent-child relationships we can learn quite a bit from what psychologists have to tell us. We can try to understand what happened to us as children, and what kind of parents we were, and we can become new, improved grandparents. In a modern setting, the bonding which takes place between the couple during the pregnancy and birth creates a much greater emotional and physical closeness—with each other and the child. We, as grandparents, have to be reschooled. Today's fathers don't teach their sons to be "brave little men," to be the strong, silent, macho types who hold back emotions and tears.

The new father figure should find his counterpart in the grandfather. Nurturing the child is now as much the father's role as it is the mother's. The authoritarian is becoming a relic. (There's much evidence that delinquent acts are a defiance against threatening father power.) Dr. Lee Salk says that "a man who cannot be affectionate with his son may be compensating for his own weak identity." The result is aloofness or an exaggerated sense of masculinity, causing both of them great harm. The part-time father who uses his career as the be-all and end-all of his workaholic existence is no longer admirable. The Victorian head of the household barely visited the nursery, would never push a baby carriage and wasn't sure he wanted to be seen walking next to one. To kiss his daughter was acceptable; to hug his son, taboo.

It makes you wonder how such unnatural relationships ever got started, and *we* should be alert to the danger of perpetuating them.

HEART SURGERY

I have often been astounded, when friends talk about their recent surgery, by how little they actually know about what was done. I suppose when we must undergo such drastic invasion of our bodies, we feel so out of control that we prefer not to know too much. Close our eyes. Be sedated. Pretend we're not there. We'd rather tell how many hours the surgeon labored and how many stitches it took to finish the job. And yet every medical team knows faster recuperation is possible when the patient and his family are well informed. The more comprehension, the less apprehension.

In 1981, more than 200,000 people had open-heart surgery in the United States. This prompted Ina Yalof to write *Open Heart Surgery,* a book which explains, in laymen's terms, precisely what is involved before, during, and after the operation. It was Benjamin Disraeli who said, "The more extensive a man's knowledge of what has been done, the greater will be his power of knowing what to do." With this quote, Ina Yalof introduces her chapter on "Preparation for Heart Surgery." It is, in fact, the motivation for this book and may

well be taken as a central thought for all dealings one
has with the medical profession.

We can take responsibility for our bodies only when
we have understanding. The better informed the patient and family about heart surgery procedure, the less
apprehensive and more realistic they'll be in their approach to preparing for surgery, the operation itself,
and follow-up care and treatment. Diagrams, illustra-
tions, and a comprehensive glossary of terms all help to
make such complicated matters part of successful recovery.

HEIRS LOOKING AT YOU

It's rare to hear of heirs who manage to divide the
estate of their parents without arguments or bad feelings. Even if surviving children have fine rapport and
in-laws (their wives and husbands) are compliant, sharing household effects and other treasures can become
contentious. "I've always had my heart set on . . . *this*
painting"; "Mother promised *me* that vase years ago";
"Those dishes match *my* set." And so on. Values—sentimental and actual—cause confusion and conflict, especially when sadness and emotional stress are added into
the mix.

On the chance that researchers on death are correct
when they claim that our spirits hang around for a
while, you *can* avoid having to "watch" these squabbles
with prudent preparations. Have an appraisal made of
your belongings, from the rug on the floor to the glass in
the cupboard. Qualified appraisers (who do nothing
else and are *not* auctioneers) are members of the Ap-

praisers Association of America or the American Society of Appraisers. They have passed stringent requirements and can be relied on for knowledge and integrity.

When these experts have researched, examined, appraised, and carefully itemized your personal effects and valuables, you have done yourself and your heirs a great service. You will know the value of your possessions. You have an acceptable document for insurance. In case of fire or theft, there is no doubt about the loss. I've heard too many sad stories of the torture people go through *after* burglary or fire, because the authorities or insurance companies make victims feel like criminals. Also, professionally appraised items are easier to sell. Or, when you want to make a gift, you have a ready dollar figure to help you decide.

But the most important advantage is to your heirs and for your peace of mind. The fee of 1 or 1 1/2 percent paid to a professional appraiser is well worth it.

HOUSEPLANTS CAN TAKE CARE OF *YOU*

Magazines are full of ads and articles that purport to have the answer to aging skin. Wrinkle creams, dry skin lotions, instant face-lifts—even soap, would you believe! As a vain woman and a professional actress, I've probably tried them all.

Aging can't be stopped. Dry air, which aggravates the problem, can. If you're heating your home in winter, chances are you're made uncomfortable by dry air. Dry air can also cause you to catch more frequent colds and make you susceptible to respiratory problems. There's a very simple solution to this which doesn't require any fancy electrical gadget or installation. It's houseplants!

The bigger the plant, the better it will serve you. And I don't mean some giant cactus that never requires your attention. Buy large plants that need *lots* of water. When you water your plants, you're watering your environment. Give a quart of water to a thirsty potted fern, and it will return it to you in the form of gently humidified air to breathe all week long. This will do wonders for your nasal passages as well as your complexion. Even the skin on the rest of your body won't get that uncomfortably itchy winter dryness.

No matter what fables you've heard about plants in the bedroom—put one or two there. You'll sleep much better.

THE INNER CLOCK

We have the preconceived notion that we function our best if we get eight hours of sleep every night. Thus we spend one third of our lives in bed!

For many older people, it's difficult to get a night of uninterrupted sleep. Waking up three or four times is often torment; and then one can't get back to sleep, just thinking about things. Fretting about the hours of so-called lost sleep causes even more tension. So we lie in bed, tossing and turning, take pills or a shot of liquor to ease ourselves back into drowsiness.

I have a suggestion if you're troubled by insomnia: if you can't sleep, *don't* just lie there counting the chimes of the clock. Get out of bed and do those things you've been meaning to do but haven't had time for. Instead of long nights, you'll gain valuable hours—iron clothes that have been sitting in your laundry basket, sew on a button, pay your bills, or write to a friend who's been waiting for a response for months. Just don't attach so much importance to what experts say about required amounts of sleep. Each of us is an individual, with a unique inner clock. And that biological clock changes from time to time. No one can tell you how much sleep you need. Even you don't know for sure.

So the next time you're staring at the ceiling in the middle of the night, put that time to good use. The inability to sleep shouldn't become a nightmare in itself. Above all, don't recount the story of your insomnia —hour by boring hour—to friends and relations. You might feel obligated to improve on it each time you tell it.

MEDICAL OPINION

Would it make you feel uncomfortable if you thought there was anything about yourself that you didn't know but others *did?*

Believe it or not, your medical history is more readily available to strangers than it is to you. As things stand now, your doctor or hospital doesn't have to release medical records to you. Your right to access to these files is *not* guaranteed by law. But a "patient may not even have to sign a release form to make that information available to a third party"—prospective employers, the military, insurance and credit companies, and federal authorities.

The medical profession, for the most part, prefers to keep things as they are. Medical records, they say, may be too technical and confusing for lay persons; perhaps doctors' opinions are of no concern to the patient or might be upsetting. But what about mistakes? Incorrect diagnoses can follow us for life. How can we correct this if we're unaware?

Information in personal medical records could be erroneous or damaging to the patient. This could be of importance in employment or insurance. Is it fair that the patient never finds out why he was turned down? *A person owns himself and everything about him.* Or does he? Your X-rays are yours. You've paid for them. Doctors, dentists, or hospitals shouldn't have the right to withhold them; at least a duplicate set, at minimal cost, should be available. When you move, want to change doctors or get additional opinions, you should be able to take all your records with you and base your decisions on information.

If the medical profession is afraid we can't handle our own medical history, *let them teach us*, in school. I propose that the AMA design a course of study for high school seniors called The Informed Medical Consumer. It may well save billions in health dollars and trillions in insurance premiums that doctors now pay to protect themselves against lawsuits.

THE MEASURE OF A MAN

What is it about retirement that shakes up a man so that he can become ill or ailing quite suddenly and unexpectedly? Harry Brod, a lecturer at the University of Southern California, points out in his course on Men and Masculinity that the strong link between work and male identity can lead to a variety of problems. He calls it the "performance principle" by which men rate themselves, on the job, in society—even in the bedroom.

Out of work, retired, a cut in salary or position, an unsatisfying job: these are the events that make a man feel powerless and erode his self-esteem. Now that men are not always the exclusive providers in many families, their position as breadwinner and authority figure in the home is no longer supreme. Men rate themselves by their paychecks. I once overheard someone say, "Making money is the most satisfying thing you can do." A change in that "measuring device" throws men a curve. Add a change in daily routine, and they have a real problem.

"Consciousness raising groups and the men's movement, in general, are doing a great deal to promote healthier definitions of masculinity," says Harry Brod. The traditional concept—that women's domain is the home—has the unfortunate side effect on men of excluding them from focusing on it as a place of importance to them, too. Men are constantly expressing a desire to be their own boss. Women *are*—at least in their homes.

Mr. Brod believes that finer distinctions need to be drawn between self-determination and domination, between assertion and aggression. An additional imbalance is created by this stereotypical denial of emotion: men are *always rational* and *only* women are *emotional*. Men need to acknowledge and deal with their emotions and should be able to express them just as women do—as honestly as possible, albeit with restraint. We will *then* be able to deal normally with each other, in interchangeable roles.

NURSING HOMES

Cuts in federal spending can be a cure or a curse. The dollars available for nursing home inspection, for instance, face sizable cuts in 1984. Does that indicate that these health care facilities for the elderly and disabled are being run better, that the industry is policing itself effectively? (Please note the word "industry," for that is what it is—a profitable one, in many cases.)

The individual states cannot provide sufficient inspectors to monitor the nursing homes within their boundaries. But even if they could, the national government may soon curtail the number of *required* annual inspections. And then there's a plan to have a private, industry-accredited organization monitor these way-stations-on-the-road-to-heaven. The fox guarding the henhouse!

"Gray gold" is what *Forbes* magazine calls the booming nursing home industry. "With the graying of America, many people will have no choice but to board their oldsters," says *Forbes*.

From where will come the long-overdue relief for this appalling situation? Nursing home reform is one of the most pressing social problems we face. There is at the moment an effort in Washington to create the *first* independent commission to inspect, evaluate, and strengthen the federal nursing home program. Reform will come only if the public realizes that we must apply pressure, remain informed, vigilant—and actively involved.

As long ago as the twelfth century, northern Europeans built beguinages—special communities of individual cottages, within the cities, built around a lovely inner courtyard garden, in which elderly women lived and devoted themselves to charitable works and to each other's needs. How civilized!

WHO CARES ABOUT NURSING HOMES

Who cares about nursing homes? Those who are already elderly, those who expect to reach that age bracket soon, those who care about someone who is old, and all who expect to be among the long-living in the future. In short, everyone.

On the "consumer" side, that is. On the supply side, the profiteers are deeply interested in this staggering statistic: one person in nine is already over sixty-five years! Three quarters of the 21,000 nursing homes are owned privately or by corporations, some of which own many hundreds of such homes, reaping enormous profits. And yet, in spite of this being an apparently limitless resource, I've seen very little competitive advertising.

Wouldn't you expect that because just one corporation owns 643 nursing homes and takes in more than a billion dollars, others would start an advertising blitz to get a better share of the market!

Perhaps nursing home corporations have trouble finding an advertising copywriter able to create a convincing sales pitch—once he's visited the establishment. Just opening the front door or stepping off the elevator on certain floors can waft a message never to be forgotten. Sounds, sights, smells to scare off the bravest! Can you visualize an ad that says: "At Sunnyvale Nursing Home your elderly are treated with reverence." "A sense of humor creates a sense of well-being." "Our guests are catered to like royalty." "Never a laundry cart in sight." "Our kitchen is only heard, seen, smelled at mealtime." "Your elderly are our guests. We treat them with utmost courtesy and love—not like naughty children." "We fill their days with pleasant activities." "Our hallways are not wheelchair parking lots."

Well, I could go on writing trumped-up creative copy. But instead I'll ask *you* to write to your congressional representative—*after* you make few unannounced visits to these human warehouses. If you find one you would be willing to live in, write to *me*.

OLD NOTIONS

Somewhere between the ages of sixteen and twenty-six, most of us take a real close look at our aims and interests. We usually take the long-range view—of about twenty-five or thirty-five years. This brings us right smack dab up to age sixty—and *that* used to be quite enough! Not anymore!

"No generation in American life has ever had to think about another thirty years of life *after* sixty. We've got to think about *sixty to ninety* now." So says Bernard Warach, author of *The Older American's Survival Guide for Better Health and a Longer Life.* I certainly agree. The opportunities and the problems of living longer are subjects for consideration from the very beginning of adulthood.

Some of what we store is excess baggage—in the attic of our minds. For those of us who are already past the midpoint of our lives, it's time to bring stored and dusty ideas out into the open—and, in many instances, discard them. How we view old age is a conditioned response, often based on notions formed in centuries other than our own.

Just take the subject of second marriage. If you and your spouse talk *openly* about it—while you're still happily together—it will not seem like betrayal to remarry later. And what is even more important, plan to take into a second marriage only that which is *you*, so that the new partner has his or her proper place and isn't "sharing" it with your former mate. If you want my opinion, no man has ever slept well in the first husband's bed, and no woman can find her way around another's kitchen. Sell it all and start a new life! Thirty more years is a long time!

SCHEMES AND SCAMS

What's black and white and read all over? Social announcements in the local paper, of course. How else would we get on all those improbable mailing lists or be confronted with solicitations and salesmen at our door? This time-tested method of communicating good—or bad—family news is no longer just a gracious social custom. An engagement, confirmation, wedding or death notification, in print with all the personal data (address included), is not a safe idea, I'm sorry to say.

You read outrageous stories daily: homes burglarized while the family is attending a joyous or sad gathering; salesmen who victimize widows by "delivering" expensive merchandise supposedly ordered by the deceased; the wedding gift that's such a great buy (supposedly an order was canceled) and it just "happens" to have the bride's initials; the vultures who come to buy your house—practically before you've returned from the funeral.

Ira Lipman, author of the book *How to Protect Yourself,* says the con artist "is a despicable criminal, preying on the uninformed and elderly, often taking their life's savings," robbing "them of both their money *and their self-respect.*"

It's not my intention to make you paranoid about the dangers that can beset you. Far from it. I'd rather you look at all these schemes and swindles with a knowing grin, and with your eyes wide open. You *know* you shouldn't buy—or sell—if you didn't *plan* to do it. No one has to tell you not to let strangers in your home—

not for a phone call, a glass of water, or any other sub-
terfuge. Purchase products only where you can return
or exchange them. Deal with services and contractors
you've checked on with neighbors or the Better Business Bureau.

Experience may be the best teacher, but *you* don't
have to be the guinea pig!

VACATION-PROOF YOUR HOME

With the pleasure of longer vacations comes the increased pressure of how to secure your house during a
long absence. The first, and most obvious, measure
against damage or burglary is neighborly cooperation.
But there are other things you can and must do.

During the weeks before leaving, create a general
checklist of preparations, including garden service or
snow removal. Make a separate list of things to do inside
and outside your home:

Inside:

Don't leave electrical appliances, especially
radios and TVs, plugged in.

Disconnect the water hose to the washing
machine.

Just before locking the door, check the
refrigerator: one rotting orange can practically
asphyxiate you after a week.

And the cupboard: one spoiled potato or onion
can be detected almost before you reopen the
front door.

The bathroom: did that toilet stop flushing?
The stove: are all the burners off, the pilot light
    safe?

Outside:
    Branches that might smash a window in a storm
        should be cut down.
    For the same reason, garden furniture should be
        stored indoors.
    Check for openings in your home, which may
        serve as an entry for rodents, including
        squirrels. Steel wool is an excellent filler for
        small spaces around water pipes.
    Every exposed pipe should be wrapped with
        insulation, especially in the garage, attic,
        basement, and crawl space.

Always remember to stand still and *listen* to your
house before you leave. Did you know you can telephone your heating system to find out how it's doing?
There's a simple, inexpensive device which plugs into
the phone jack. If the temperature in your house should
fall below, say, 40 degrees, you'll get a busy signal when
you call your own number. You can then alert a friend
who has a key. There's no simpler way to protect frozen
pipes which could burst.

There are many devices to deter burglars, some very
costly and complicated, some simple and perhaps
equally effective. Lights, inside and out, controlled by a
timer, are good protection because thieves prefer darkness. Windows and doors can usually be made more
secure: better locks, double or triple glass, braces for
sliding doors, metal grilles on basement windows.
Alarm systems help, too, but are no guarantee. Ade-

quate, updated insurance coverage can give you peace of mind.

So, be prepared, and enjoy your vacation without worry. Isn't that what you're after when you take a vacation?

THE SHRINKING OF AMERICA

We live in an age in which solutions are expected for absolutely every problem. If the car doesn't work, we take it to a mechanic. If the cat is listless, we call the vet. The child who misbehaves has to see a psychologist. Couples who can't get along engage separate divorce lawyers. There is a medication not only for every physical ailment but for every psychic one, too. We are not supposed to suffer—even temporarily. And, most of all, we expect to find a so-called professional to help us get past every obstacle.

If we pay for advice—and do we ever!—we tend to exaggerate the benefits, especially from psychological therapy. Some studies have been made which are said to prove that people who *don't* seek professional help by a trained therapist may overcome their difficulties equally well in the same amount of time, by being in touch with friends or talking it out with a religious leader.

In the opinion of psychologist Bernie Zilbergeld, who wrote *The Shrinking of America*, "the most common products of most therapies are not behavior change, but caring, comforting and structuring." He feels that professionals may not get better results than amateur advisers. Apparently, techniques in therapy are less important than the rapport between the patient and the counselor. Perhaps the main difference between a friend and a therapist is that the latter sits and listens, mostly in silence, at approximately $2 a minute, while the friend will feel obliged to ameliorate your anxieties by playing the game of one-upmanship by telling you what happened to *him* and how awful it was. Of course, there are equally elaborate studies which support the theory that psychotherapy has phenomenal results. Zilbergeld's basic advice to patients undergoing therapy is: accept yourself as you are, but work on your problems. The chief benefit of therapy seems to come from the rapport between two human beings.

It all comes down to caring and comforting—those things we *can* give to each other.

WIDOWHOOD

"You *will* eventually feel better," is the reassuring message conveyed to the bereaved in the booklet *Coping With Widowhood,* by the Baltimore City Commission on Aging. "It might take up to two years to adjust to your changed life, and the stages of bereavement won't be easy. The numbness experienced at first may be followed by bursts of anger, profound sadness, indecisiveness, restlessness, an inability to concentrate, and, sometimes, an acute awareness of your own mortality."

Your world has been turned upside down. We are all completely unprepared for this massive trauma. There are, however, ways both to accept and combat these normal feelings. If you're restless, for example, "adapt to your restlessness." Leaf through magazines instead of tackling a weighty novel, and don't feel you have to stay at social gatherings all evening. And use as much physical energy as possible—swim, hike, take long walks.

Widowers should pat themselves on the back frequently as they master the chores their wives used to do. And if they feel sad in the middle of an empty house, one much-needed reminder may be helpful: crying is therapeutic, whether you're a man or a woman. Make your family and friends part of your life. Learn how to ask for help, and don't fear you're intruding. The more practical aspects of widowhood include dealing with funeral arrangements, legal help, Social Security benefits, disposing of personal effects, and money management. Be sure to get competent advice.

The booklet concludes on a positive note: "Widowhood doesn't have to mean 'The End.' " It can mean the beginning of a new life for men and women, with special challenges and rewards.

"TOUGHLOVE"

Most of us are a product of the times in which we were raised. Early training and attitudes endure. Mind set, I think it's called. I have a friend who lived only the first ten years of her life abroad but, even in middle age, finds it easier to do multiplication and the alphabet in her mother tongue. We neither forget nor transcend early teachings.

It takes conscious thought to be part of the present. Grandparenting is where we are likely to make the effort. For instance, how shall we behave toward youngsters who are difficult? Many young parents have serious conflicts with children who can't conform to acceptable family standards: tough kids, unmanageable behavior, unprintable language, disrupting the household and undermining the family structure.

Parents are learning about a new approach to interaction with such kids. A few years ago a Pennsylvania couple, David and Phyllis York, who are professional counselors, came up with a method of helping parents with hard-to-handle kids. They call it Toughlove. For mothers and fathers who've lost control over their children—who are being used, abused, manipulated, and pushed around—this approach becomes an anchor in the storm.

From the Yorks comes the theory that the excessive freedom and unconditional love we *think* we owe at all times can be toughened once we learn to *believe* in our rights. In other words, tough rules, *with* love:

> Take control and don't weaken.
> Look the other way, if you've been looking too
>   close.
> Yell, if you've been too calm.
> Calm down, if you've screamed too much.
> Make demands, if you've been reticent.
> Ignore them, if you've been too involved.
> Push back, if you've been pushed around.

We grandparents, as visitors or surrogates, must learn to take our cues from the parents in order not to undermine their authority.

PERSONAL SUPPORT SYSTEM

Living alone—at any age—can be hazardous to your health. There are obvious side effects, such as loneliness (which can be depressing), or undisciplined eating habits (which can cause malnutrition). A very real health hazard can be a sudden illness or accident, with no one there to help.

At least one chapter of the American Red Cross is trying to do something about this. The Fairfax, Virginia, chapter gives a course in self-preservation for those who live alone. It is called Develop Your Personal Health Support System. This one-time two-hour course advises single residents on the precautions they should take for themselves, and to be alert to the need of *others*. For instance, if newspapers accumulate on the doormat, or the dog barks longer than usual, or the lawn didn't get watered, or the lights didn't go on—be a neighbor! Be nosy! Become involved!

Individualism, privacy, fear, and too many other hands-off, eyes-averted attitudes are the basis for noninvolvement among us. We're also afraid or embarrassed to seek help. The elderly lady who asked directions to the avenue she was walking *away* from became so flustered and apologetic, she felt a need to say, "I'm always doing stupid things like that."

People who live alone must organize their own support system—friends, relatives, and organizations they can call on. Be sure that your home is so organized that a helpful neighbor can find what is needed for your benefit—medications, special instructions, names and phone numbers (paste a legible list on the bathroom mirror).

Don't wait; organize your personal support system today!

TIES THAT BIND

When children become adults and have families of their own, relationships with *their* parents often need more breathing space. Feeling obligated to call an aging parent *every day* isn't very rewarding—for either party. Those "duty" visits every Friday or every holiday can be a drag.

How can it be arranged for the child to perform according to expectation and keep in touch with his parents? One way is to take turns: husband, wife, other siblings, grandchildren, nieces, nephews can, if necessary, take an assigned number and alternate calls and visits. Such a plan of sharing is beneficial to all. The grandchildren will learn a great deal of compassion and understanding from this contact with the elderly; the middle generation will feel less pressure; and the old will get a more varied look at the outside world.

Grandparents who expect the whole gang for Thanksgiving or Christmas—no excuses accepted— aren't aware that they are *making demands* instead of just offering hospitality and togetherness. They, the older generation, aren't the only ones who are a family; the younger marrieds (with or without children) are also families, trying to build a backlog of memories and traditions. It's the logical transition from one generation to the next. But neither loyalty nor devotion should be akin to millstones.

It's not easy for some of us to let go. But it can be worked at. If you search your memory a little, you'll see that you had to do it, too, in order to break away.

NATURAL TRANQUILIZERS

Most of us have our own way of handling tension and anxiety. The man who slams out of the house and goes for a long walk to avoid arguments happens to be doing the right thing. So does the woman who decides this is the moment to take down the curtains and wash the windows. The youngster who escapes from school or parental pressure by batting a ball against the house for an hour is also on the right track to tranquilizing his mental agitation *without* drugs.

Valium and other drugs of that type used to be prescribed like aspirin, with total disregard for possible side effects and withdrawal symptoms. It is not the safe and risk-free drug it was once thought to be. Patients who attempt gradual withdrawal from Valium, even under medical supervision, often develop extreme distress.

There is great concern about the risk of addiction to Valium and similar drugs consumed on a regular basis. Withdrawal symptoms include tremors, dizziness, insomnia, and other discomforts. If you're all saying to yourselves that this doesn't concern you, you only "take a little," only "now and then," then who is consuming four billion doses of prescription tranquilizers at a cost of two billion dollars a year?

The best "prescription" against anxiety and tension is physical exercise. Yes, a long walk, scrubbing the floor, throwing a bowling ball, or cutting the lawn is as effective as any tranquilizing drug—and has only beneficial aftereffects, at a price you can't beat. It's always available, you can't run out of it, no one can use it up before you get your hands on it. You don't have to hide it or horde it. It can't kill you or cause mental aberrations. And yes, you will become addicted. Now isn't that nice!

The handsome young environmentalist who looks after my trees is going into modeling now and hopes for a theatrical career. His nature-inspired calm personality is a novelty among his new co-workers in the so-called glamour industry. For myself, I think my explosive Irish family gave me the means to conquer stress. You can't possibly compete with that much shouting and temperamental behavior; it rolls right past you when you've grown up with it.

SLEEPING PILL HABITS

Are you thinking of kicking the sleeping pill habit? Withdrawing from the ranks of the estimated one in four Americans who at times rely on sleeping pills to speed slumber should be done slowly and carefully, under medical supervision. "Sleeping pill users can build strong psychological and biological addictions to these drugs," says Dr. Elliot Phillips, director of the Sleep Disorder Center at Holy Cross Hospital in a suburb of Los Angeles. By reducing the dosage *slowly*, mental and physical withdrawal symptoms should be less severe. Most of these symptoms will have ceased by the end of a two- to three-week period.

In his work Dr. Phillips has helped many patients to give up sleeping pills. He's found that it's easier for patients who realize that sleeping pills are not a wonder drug. "No sleeping pills will produce natural sleep," he says. At best they may reduce by a third the amount of time it takes to fall asleep. For example, a person who normally takes an hour to fall asleep may find that a pill reduces the time to forty minutes. Anyone who takes a sleeping pill and falls soundly asleep when his head hits the pillow could probably just as well have taken a sugar pill. He would have enjoyed the same result—without any morning-after grogginess.

"Sleeping pills have not been shown to be effective for more than four weeks of nightly use," says the doctor. After that, as a result of the body's growing dependency on them, they only prevent withdrawal. So it hardly seems worth the money, danger, and side effects.

I have my own system: a couple of soda crackers, eaten ever so slowly, while I read in bed. A pleasant book—Russell Baker or *Blue Highways,* a story in the *Smithsonian* magazine or *National Geographic*—will soothe me into sleeping like a baby.

DIET AND JET LAG

As the world shrinks, so must our stomachs. We, and Superman, can travel at the speed of a bullet. I can make up my mind to be in London three hours from

now; but don't ask me what my body will say about it
when I get there!

The biological clock in every one of our cells is regu-
lated by the time zone in which we live. Traveling at
1,200 miles per minute, we are zipping along much
faster than the physical system can adapt. Crossing the
continent on the Twentieth Century Limited may have
been slow by comparison, but it was a lot easier on the
internal workings of the traveler. While twenty-first-
century engineers conjure faster and faster transportation, scientists research ways to make it easier on passengers. They have found that jet lag *can* be minimized
to help avoid enervating symptoms, such as insomnia,
digestive disturbance, water retention, tenseness.

A laboratory in Illinois has devised a "feast and fast"
diet to help intercontinental travelers avoid the disori-
entation and discomfort of jet lag. According to Dr.
Charles Ehret, fasting on the day of travel is very beneficial. It helps the body adjust to time-zone changes. For
longer distance travel, he suggests a three-day regimen
of alternating days of feasting and fasting. On "feast"
days, a high-protein diet is recommended—lots of
meat, chicken, eggs, and high-protein cereals. To stimulate sleep on feast days, the last meal of the day should
also contain high-carbohydrate foods, such as pasta and
legumes. "Fast" days do not mean total abstinence, but
your intake should be less than 700 calories.

It may be a good idea to keep to such a regimen for
the duration of the journey. It gives us a chance to enjoy
the good food of the place we're visiting and puts us
back on schedule when we get home.

For people who are not used to drinking alcohol at
odd hours, the free or inexpensive bar service on planes
can be very seductive and spell disaster. If you can't

pass up the bargain, put the little bottle in your pocket and enjoy it under more normal circumstances.

CAREGIVERS

We are given no training in being caregivers. People over the age of forty or fifty (the children of today's aged population) had no real examples to watch as they matured; no role models who would prepare them for the eventual job of being responsible for their own parents. This country was still very mobile in the years between the wars; young people moved away from their hometowns, leaving the elderly behind. In many cases parents remained in the "old country" while their children sought independence in America.

This, then, was the beginning of the nuclear family: a nucleus of one set of parents and a few kids—no grandmother, spending her last years; no grandfather, puttering about the house; no one to honor, revere, respect, or learn to tolerate. And, of course, people didn't live as long as they do today.

More and more people at the age of sixty-five, ready and eager to retire and have some fun, suddenly find themselves with a parent in their care who is perhaps eighty-five years old—physically, financially, emotionally dependent on them in every way. Unless we, in a changing society, recognize and address ourselves to this problem—for that is what it is—almost every family will soon find itself in an untenable situation, which will drown their chance at personal happiness.

Fortunately, there are group efforts that can help teach and support the family as caregivers to the elderly. The National Support Center for Families of the Aging, in Swarthmore, Pennsylvania, is one such program, teaching families communication skills and problem-solving techniques to better cope with caregiving duties.

Growing old, really old, is part of life, more now than ever before. Life goes on, and we must help each other do the best we can—for the old, but also for their younger relatives.

WIDOWERS

Men do not expect to outlive their wives. That generalization doesn't apply to every husband; statistically, though, older widowed men are an especially vulnerable group.

A study conducted by the researchers at Johns Hopkins University found that a husband's death had almost no effect on the mortality rate of women; but not so the other way around. Older men are more likely to die within several years of their wives' death, in far greater numbers than married men of the same age. Most men never contemplate living alone. Traditionally, women do. They have dozens of role models—among their acquaintances in later life and among their relatives in early childhood. Their province is the home; it doesn't frighten them to be managing it on their own. Men are quite unprepared to find themselves alone; statistics, they thought, had been stacked against this possibility.

Women know how to cry; men internalize their grief. This, too, makes them much more susceptible to heart disease and ill health as a result of their bereavement.

In good marriages, the man often relies entirely on his life's companion for emotional support, as a sounding board, and as the recipient of his private thoughts and confidences. Most women have at least one other person with whom they share such a relationship.

One of the great revelations for an older man who suddenly finds himself widowed is the concept of dependency. Here he's gone through life imagining that his wife was totally dependent on him. Suddenly he realizes that he was equally dependent on her—in all those everyday matters which he now finds so overwhelming.

So, men remarry. And that is as it should be. It's easier for them because there are so many unmarried women. I just wish they would choose among *their* age group, and leave the young things to *their* peers.

HEARING LOSS

When the President dons a hearing aid, he's not betraying a weakness; he's showing a strength. By his action he says it's perfectly all right to have a disability. President Franklin Roosevelt, on the other hand, didn't let the public know for a long time that he had paralysis.

Fighting as hard as we can against a disability is essential; we don't want to give in and give up. But denying it, for reasons of pride or prejudice, is a whole other matter. Many people, especially the elderly, don't like to admit to hearing loss and would rather suffer than succumb. Not hearing well enough is debilitating *and* dangerous. It's a strain on the nervous system—to follow a conversation, watch television, attend theater, or make phone calls; out in the street it can be lethal.

Even at home not hearing the sound of a boiling pot or the crackle of the broiler can cause problems for the twenty million people in this country who are hearing impaired. Only about 12 percent of them wear hearing aids. Devices have existed since the horn grandmother held to the ear when I was a child. The most technologically advanced units are so compact that they're virtually unnoticeable and are very durable, with amplifiers the size of a pencil point, weighing only a couple of grams.

The potential consumer must exercise some caution, though; most important is the careful choice of a doctor to diagnose the degree and type of deafness. In choosing a suitable device, test the quality of sound. Be certain it works for you in quiet as well as noisy surroundings. Is it comfortable to wear and easy to control? Price and upkeep costs must also be considered. Perhaps it is wise to rent before you buy. And if you're not sure where and what to buy and what the going prices are, ask the Better Business Bureau in your area.

DECISIONS, DECISIONS!

Strange as it may seem, we all learn to make decisions. We even comprehend that good, bad, or indifferent, the results are *our* responsibility. The clever parent allows for these successes and failures early, encouraging self-reliance and self-worth. Somehow, in our retirement years, many of us begin to doubt our own ability or, even, our right to decision making. Failure or

incompetence looms more menacing, perhaps because rectifying mistakes may take more time than we think we have. But something can be done about that outlook.

First of all, try as much as you can to continue to make decisions. Just be sure to base your judgment on facts. Take time to acquaint yourself with all aspects of the plan. Next, admit when you feel less than qualified and seek competent advice. Neither pride nor embarrassment should stand in our way. Reliance on a second or even a third opinion is the best way to cope with the complexities of financial, social, or medical decision making.

On a recent trip to California, I had a bit of sciatica to cope with. My friends rushed me off to a doctor. The doctor wanted to rush me off to the hospital. But me, I hustled down to the airport and flew home. There, of course, I went to bed for a nice, therapeutic rest. The decisions were all mine and I was satisfied. The only one that gave me a bit of a problem was the decision to *get up again.* You know how it is; there comes a time when you really have to say, "Get up, old girl," or you run the risk of making the bed your habitat.

Jack Smith, the syndicated columnist, calls what I do "aging gracefully." I thank him for the compliment. And I pass it on to you. We can all do that—age gracefully—if we work on it a little.

PUT-DOWNS

Think about how many times a day we all make misguided, self-sacrificing, or self-deprecating statements.

Usually what we *mean* is not what we say. What we say
about ourselves, which is meant to sound humble or shy
or sensitive, is often motivated by altogether different
reasons. If we criticize our housekeeping, we are probably trying to build our self-importance and "busy-life"
image. When we put down our appearance or wardrobe, we may be seeking compliments. Self-criticism
can be a means of avoiding responsibility. "I can't do a
thing right" may just be a cover-up for laziness. But
some type of self-effacing behavior can actually be
quite effective in improving performance.

When I first started my radio program, I was very
critical of my delivery and my voice, even though I
have heard myself in countless films and recordings. I
became more sensitive to the subtle changes I wanted
to make to do it better. The self-put-downs we *must*
avoid are those which freeze us—make us unable to
function. It's okay to be tough on yourself, if that's what
it takes to get the job done. An inferiority complex, on
the other hand, can be stifling.

Psychologists advise us to examine our own words
and actions to see whether self-imposed pressures actually are helping us perform better or, possibly, not at all
—without even giving it a try. Sometimes setting a goal
of absolute perfection results in a complete shutdown,
because, obviously, perfection is impossible.

The older we get, the more likely we are to make
frequent negative statements about ourselves. Perhaps
what we are really seeking is reassurance that we're
loved, that we're needed.

PSYCHONEUROIMMUNOLOGY

The three-hundred-year-old philosophical theory that the mind is totally separate from the body is getting a thorough overhauling in modern research labs. Recognizing the link between mind and disease is as old as tribal medicine but has a tongue-twisting new name, which took me one whole day of practice to pronounce: *psychoneuroimmunology.* It's not black magic. Psychosomatic ailments *are* real, not imagined. Placebos *do* work.

We all remember from our school days those experiments in conditioning by the Russian physiologist Pavlov, which have long been accepted as the first in the field. He demonstrated that the body will respond to mental stimulation. If I say to you "lemon juice," you probably can feel a change in your mouth, a tingling, can't you? Scientists are making great strides in understanding how this works. Eventually it will help us to fight disease, to stay well. We have learned, for instance, that great and continued stress or shock lowers the immunological activity of the body, making us susceptible to illness.

At the Ontario Cancer Research Institute, scientific work shows that "conditioning can enhance, as well as depress, immune activity." Stress can apparently be responsible for both negative and positive action of the immune system. Although disease is caused by many factors—genetics, environment, infection, and so on—there's less and less doubt about the effect of psychological influences.

According to the magazine *Psychology Today,* "Bernard Fox, of the National Cancer Institute, says that psychological factors affect the probability of a person's getting cancer." Mental processes change the body chemistry. If the roses on the wallpaper make you sneeze, don't worry that you're losing your mind. On the contrary! It's hard at work on your immune system. Similarly, it's not just the chicken soup but *how* and by whom it's served that make you feel better.

Positive attitudes—optimism, high self-esteem, an outgoing nature, joyousness, and the ability to cope with stress—when established early in life, may be the most important basis for continued good health.

LOSS OF INNOCENCE

This is not the first time in history that children are treated as adults and virtually stripped of their childhood. In the agrarian days and in the beginning of the Industrial Revolution, children were an important part of the labor force. Child mortality and the much briefer life span compressed the life cycle. Neither playing nor learning was considered sufficiently important to warrant decades of attention or devotion.

Sad to say, the more things change, the more they seem to regress. Ours is a new age of loss of innocence. There's not much in the adult world that small children are not privy to—whether political, moral, scientific, sexual, or emotional. Children's television programs vie for viewing with programs highlighting war, crime, sex, perversion, aberration, horror, intrigue.

To some of us, home entertainment still means hav-

ing friends visit and, perhaps, sit down to a meal together. But that's changing, too—if and when it takes
place at all. People who have children are now carting
them along on visits to friends and relatives—unin-
vited! There are many reasons for this, not the least of
which is that they don't see their offspring as *children,*
and don't see them often enough. They drag them
along out of a sense of guilt—for having left them alone
while Mom and Pop are at work. Sitters, if available, are
barely affordable, and, with today's mores, a risky
choice for companionship. It might also be that parents
are "hiding" behind their children; tots usually domi-
nate the scene, channeling conversation, and adult interchange becomes banal.

Grandparents, as we all know, are in the frontline of
this invasion. A word of advice: define the boundaries of
your social life and expect to defend them.

SHARED HOUSING

Just as I walked past two elderly people, one said,
"But dear, my *children* are senior citizens." This
charming statement serves to illustrate the statistics we
keep reading about the "elder generation explosion."
Since we're all living longer, the age-old question of
where to live has become a national topic. I'm happy to
know that some very interesting and worthwhile solutions are becoming quite plausible.

To be independent is the first prerequisite for those
elderly people who are still in fairly good health. They
all have two needs in common: pleasant surroundings
and protection from loneliness. Many older men and

women end up in nursing homes or other such facilities merely because they thought there were no alternatives. Responsibilities overwhelm them. Financial insecurity limits their lives. Loneliness depresses them. Fear of illness or crime drives them into despair.

Sharing homes is the new way the elderly are escaping the trap of retreating into institutions. Abraham Lurie, director of social work at Long Island Jewish Hillside Medical Center, says, "We are using *existing* housing, providing the elderly with necessary services, and making it possible for frail elderly to *live together* and *stay* in the community." In Long Island, New York, the counties provide seed money for shared living quarters in garden apartments. Rent paid by the residents helps with upkeep, housekeeping, maid service, support from social workers, and those who can't make it on their own.

The men and women who share apartments or private homes know that they'll have to be tolerant toward each other—pretty much the way any family has to be. That is *just* what they gain from community living arrangements: a new family of their own.

RELOCATION

For many older people who have lived in the same neighborhood for years, the prospect of moving is frightening. Even if the area has gone down, you'd probably feel more comfortable remaining in less desirable surroundings than, say, becoming a less desired resident in a new community or moving in with younger relatives.

Sudden uprooting is usually an unforeseen result of losing a life partner, and it can be a big, irreversible mistake. We should maintain our independence as long as possible, because it is the key to self-respect. Most of us hesitate to discuss how we view our future with our children—*before* it becomes a matter of importance. We should understand our own feelings and make our children privy to them.

How you want to handle your own affairs—now and later on (when you may be less able)—shouldn't be a taboo subject. Your children are just as confused and overwhelmed by these problems as you are. It is best to discuss them with a sense of ease and openness, *now*. Talking about them after the fact won't be nearly as productive.

There are many options. Periodic visits, for a week or so at a time, are usually more therapeutic for all concerned than a permanent living arrangement, whether together *or* alone. Don't forget to consider the inevitable nagging guilt feelings that cloud the relationship between parent and child. Frank talk is the best insurance against disagreeable and stressful living conditions.

Much of what your children believe is directly due to your influence as a parent. This is true, also, of their attitude toward aging!

ONCE UPON A TIME

The first children to have had the misfortune to be brought up on television entertainment are today's young parents. I wonder if they know how to tell their children a make-believe, old-fashioned story.

If TV programming governs the timetable of a family, is there even a moment left in which to tell a story? Around the dinner table, with dessert, would be a good time slot—*if* it's not already allotted for viewing. Of course, there is bedtime; but, alas, not if the last allowed program is crowding the hour.

"Once upon a time . . ." How that used to put the little noses up and quiet the room down. In our house, the evening ritual was an ongoing tale called "The Further Adventures of Minnie Weisenpfeffer." To those of you who don't know just how to tell a story—and to those of us who did it for decades and have forgotten—I'll give a few pointers.

> Try as hard as you can *not* to teach (says this
> teacher) while telling a story—no morals, no
> preachments, no references to "good little
> boys and girls."
> Make it exciting, adventurous, silly, funny, cute,
> and just a touch theatrical.
> Change your voice a bit for each character. Put
> in highs and lows, sound effects, pauses. There
> should be emotion, but not so much the child
> won't be able to sleep.
> Involve your little audience with ". . . and what
> do you think happened then?" That way you'll
> find out how his mind works and you'll be
> able to gear the story to his understanding.
> The child could even play one of the
> characters to keep him interested and
> fantasizing.

That is the key—mental stimulation and activated imagination! No child to whom a story is being told on a one-to-one basis ever looks like a zonked-out zombie, the way little TV viewers do. The best time to practice your art as a storyteller is—well—anytime: bedtime, sick time, travel time, dinnertime. Don't you think it's high time?

MOM AND POP

Is there life after parenthood? In most cases, about thirty to fifty years! That's a very long time for two sets of adults—parents and grown children—to play a role that nature once intended to last no more than a dozen years. When young marrieds each get a set of in-laws and are henceforth supposed to call them Mother and Father, they find it very difficult at first. Doesn't it make sense to call these new relatives by their given names?

Perhaps we should be on a first-name basis with our own parents at that age. It's illogical to be someone's "child" for life, just as it's unreasonable to play the parental role toward independent adults and family units. Older people think of themselves as the basis of a family—the trunk of the tree, as it were. But who put them there? Didn't they have parents?

Why is it such a shock that each generation sees *itself* as a beginning, not a branch! To become friends with your children requires abdication as a parent. That job should only have lasted about eighteen years. A lot of uncomfortable and uncalled-for guilt on both sides can be avoided. We don't tell our friends how *they* should act or look. We don't get involved in *their* finances. We don't criticize *them* for their beliefs or their private lives. Why, then, continue parenting thirty-, forty-, fifty-year-olds? Your child can be your friend, and you can be his or hers.

It may make it a lot easier for everyone concerned if you suggest that your children call you by your first name now. After all, they did stop saying "Mommy" and "Daddy" at one point. The only relationship we seem to want to continue in an unaltered state is precisely the one which we can't expect to—parent and child!

KEEP YOUR COOL

Just as a pet is sure to find the warmest spot in the house in winter, you can rely on a cat or dog to show you the coolest place in summer—stretched out on the floor. A heat wave is particularly debilitating for older people, especially those with circulatory or heart problems. Use of certain drugs, such as tranquilizers and diuretics, will also increase strain on the body during hot weather.

Before the days of air-conditioning, one effective cooling method was cross ventilation. No one talks about that anymore, but it does move stuffy air by creating a draft. Closing the windows and pulling down opaque shades on the sunny side in the morning, and on the opposite side, in the afternoon, helps to keep some of the heat out. A fan will circulate the air, and the darkness creates an illusion of coolness. No doubt some of the discomfort we feel is mental. "Isn't it a hot day!" said all too plaintively and too often can actually make you feel worse.

If you must go out, do it early or late in the day. If

there's no way to cool your home, go to a public place—
a library, movie, or department store. Take it easy.
Walk slowly, in the shade, on the streets with the least
traffic. Buses, trucks, and cars raise the street temperature many degrees. Wear natural, light-colored fabrics,
like cotton, very loose-fitting to permit evaporation of
perspiration. That, as we all know, is the body's cooling
system, which must be allowed to function freely; be
sure to supply the needed liquids to let it work. Ask
your doctor how to replace the sodium chloride you
lose. Taking cool baths or letting cold water run over
the wrists and wetting the earlobes does help; these are
not just old wives' tales. But don't use modern antiper-
spirant deodorants. Regular ones are quite sufficient.
Rich foods and alcohol strain the body unnecessarily.
Remember that calories *are* heat. Summer is a good
time to cut down.

JOB INTERVIEWS

Job hunting in the middle years is becoming an ever-
increasing phenomenon. The economy is reshuffling a
lot of workers and executives; and many people are
seeking second careers or, in the case of older women,
first careers outside the home.

It isn't easy to prepare yourself for the emotional
strain of looking for a job and facing interviews.
Chances are that the interviewer hates it as much as
you do. If you've ever been the interviewer, you know
that you're almost as uncomfortable as the applicant.
You, as a seasoned adult, can take advantage of that by
trying to make the potential employer feel at ease.

Whatever you do, don't make much of your age or of the age difference between you. When you build your image, do it in a straightforward manner, neither self-deprecatingly nor glowingly. Talk about *current* accomplishments, talents, and credits—not your world-shaking discovery of two decades ago. Whatever your reason for seeking employment, *try not to complain.*

Neither your relationship with your former employer nor your personal finances are of interest. Don't try to bolster your image by playing hard-to-get. If you can start Monday, say so. If the salary isn't unreasonable, accept it, with a proviso for an early review. That's much better than putting on insulted airs. I've heard it said that being one of the later interviewees rather than the first gives you a better chance. The employer doesn't really get his mind on the subject until he sees he's running down toward the bottom of the list and hopes the want ad will pay out.

First impressions are crucial—how you sound, look, walk, sit, listen, and *what* you say in the first few minutes. Believe it or not, the applicant doesn't really have to do all the talking. The person on the other side of the desk will often sell *you* the job. You may very well be letting *him* talk *you* into accepting.

HOT FLASH

A report is getting around that women who eat a lot less meat but more vegetable and fiber are not as likely to have breast cancer. In those societies where meat and fat are a small part of the diet, statistics for this disease are much lower. We Westerners—those of us who aren't vegetarians—still have a great deal to learn about the connection between nutrition and health.

In any case, all women should routinely examine themselves at least once a month, no matter what age they are. If your doctor has never shown you how to examine for breast cancer properly yourself, ask him or stop in at a clinic. You can also write to the local American Cancer Society for a booklet which will teach you this simple, effective *lifesaving* technique. Women who become ill are said to have a tendency to blame themselves for their problems. Now *why* do we do that! It's true that our biological makeup throws us curves with unending regularity, but that's no reason to become self-conscious about our physical or mental health.

Hormonal changes *do* affect us—body and mind. So be it. Menopause and the accompanying inner and outer manifestations shouldn't stigmatize us, shame us, depress us, or be shrouded in fear and silence. Nature intended it! We should neither fan the fires of embarrassment nor perpetuate the myth that it's the living end to everything. It's time to get past the notion that mere survival is all we expect of ourselves and foster, instead, a positive approach to aging.

HOME HEALTH CARE

Economists know that skyrocketing prices come equipped with a built-in cure: namely, reduced demand. In simplistic terms, recent oil price history serves to illustrate this; conservation and alternatives became the order of the day. I wonder if this will eventually be the way health care will cure its ills.

In large city hospitals it now costs approximately $340 a day just to keep a patient in bed. Unfortunately, there are far too many elderly Medicare patients who cannot be released, when logically they should be sent home to recuperate. If they have no one who can help care for them, and if they refuse nursing home care or cannot be accommodated there, they stay in hospitals, sometimes for additional weeks or months.

In New York City an experimental home health care program is worth watching, a program launched by The Lutheran Medical Center and New York City's Planning Commission. On a small scale, they train unemployed welfare mothers to be home attendants for seven hours a day to elderly recuperating patients. Medical equipment is provided when needed, and doctors and therapists make frequent house calls.

Does it sound expensive? Remember, one hospital bed, occupied, costs Medicare $340 a day. Nursing homes are a bargain at $80 a day. But this experimental home care program would apparently help to solve the problem at $60 a day. Seven hours, of course, isn't twenty-four hours. But many patients can manage alone, or with the help of neighbors or their relatives who work during the day. I'm sure recovery is faster in our own surroundings than shut away in a hospital. And what about the benefit to the unemployed welfare recipient? She receives more than free training. She gains self-respect. So would *men,* if they were to be included. I think it all makes a great deal of sense.

FUNERALS

Nature puts a beginning and an end to everything. We shouldn't feel so devastated by that thought. In the film *On Golden Pond*, Katharine Hepburn makes the discovery that there *is* finality and that acceptance can fill the time remaining with *life*. Everything that lives must wither and die. We are all united with all the other animals, plants, and organisms.

It makes you wonder, therefore, why so many people will pay their last dollar for an impregnable, lead-lined, polished mahogany, white-satin-upholstered casket, with solid brass fittings, in which to place their embalmed remains. Why not a plain pine box and a shroud? I'd much prefer that money were spent on the living. New York's Councilman Henry Stern maintains that "aside from a house or a car, a funeral is the single most expensive purchase that many people make." Some states are now writing very stringent rules about the practices of funeral homes.

Even though it's very difficult to monitor the funeral business, such a practice would, perhaps, open the eyes of people to our strange customs and to the blatant violations of the "selling" aspect of this solemn business. It is, for instance, often illegal to require coffins for cremations. Nor is embalming to be performed unless asked for.

It's time that we begin to look at our own finality not as a kind of failure but as a natural consequence of life. Memories, especially those which deal with loss or pain, *should* weaken with time. To forget is more normal than to dwell on sadness. It is a healthy response to allow the details of sad events to fade and become less compelling. To honor the memory of someone we cherish is in no way connected with the elaborate display at a funeral.

FLIRTATION

Do mature people still flirt? The best part of being at a social gathering used to be what was called innocent flirtation. Whispered compliments, ego boosting, in words or looks, not necessarily meant to lead to anything serious. It was just a way of exercising sexuality mentally in order to feel good about yourself and about the "party of the second part." The result was a lovely glow and euphoria that you could *take home* and apply to the relationship with the one who lived there with you.

This predates loveless sex and drug-induced highs. Which sure dates me and, perhaps, you, too. "Words! Words! Words!" screams Eliza Dolittle at her suitor in *My Fair Lady*. But to my way of thinking, words are in too short supply between men and women. It's *all right* to tell someone how sexy she looks, even if you're both in your later years. What's more, there's nothing wrong with showing how pleased you are to hear it.

The best kind of flirting doesn't have much to do with the body. Especially at our age, we would all be more pleased to be told how witty we are, that our ideas are stimulating, or that we move gracefully. *Tell him* he's fantastic! *(Why* you think so is irrelevant.) It makes both of you feel great! "Romance" is a word not much in vogue these days. But you should certainly remember it, as I do. I think perhaps people wouldn't have to come on so strong if some gallant remark smooths the way. You feel appreciated; you can relax your eagerness to be noticed.

Flirtation is a sport; you've got to exercise it to stay in trim. It is also the gentle art of making someone feel pleased with himself. Flirtation is primarily a device for gaining attention without intention.

Part 2

*If there were no daily problem
solving, life would be a bowl
of pabulum.*

LONG MARRIAGES

Winning isn't everything. It's the *only* thing . . . *to avoid!* That replay of the old sports axiom is one view of long-term marriages. Researchers are busily poking into why and how marriage can last into the high numbers—as long as forty-five or fifty-five years. What causes the focus of attention on "golden sunset" marriages is longevity—people living eighty or ninety years —and doing it *together* if they've learned the ways and means of peaceful coexistence.

One of the most basic commandments is Don't try to win. Exchanging ideas is the direct opposite of convincing the opponent. If people could just learn to listen to each other and leave the discussion with a happy phrase like, "I suppose that's one way of looking at it"— well then, they'd have made it. Marriages that work can last twenty or thirty years *after* the children have gone off on their own. That's a long time. Unless your aim is to win a medal as a survivor, you had better find out how to be good friends.

A second commandment is role relaxing—that is, *no* rigid rules about male/female duties, tasks, or activities. There's much more cooperation and common interest between couples who "mix 'n' match" their activities. *Shared* decision making is the more modern approach, now that women are no longer regarded as dependent, ineffectual clinging vines. That means equal power—in other words, no power play.

Mutual respect and admiration are what you'll find in

long-lasting marriages. Perhaps those are the people
who learned early in life that marriage is not a fifty-fifty
proposition—that only 100 percent from *each* of them
can possibly make it work.

GUILT

What does a guilt feeling do to you? It can wake you
up in the middle of the night and make you wonder if
your bike is out in the rain—even though you haven't
owned one for fifty years. It can cause a divorce because
a prenuptial dalliance has made you unresponsive. But
it *also* keeps you from driving through red lights, taking
the coins off the news counter, or cheating your business partner.

Guilt is good and bad. We don't come equipped with
it. Babies aren't born with it. We're all taught it—in
varying degrees, depending on the society that nur-
tures us. Older members of the clan play a large part in
the process of teaching and perpetuating the best *and*
the worst of it. All the more reason for us to inform
ourselves—on a continuing basis—on what is right and
wrong with guilt. Much of it is destructive. Some of it is
essential. Where do we draw the line?

It's not astonishing that today there's more crime,
drug and alcohol abuse, and other antisocial behavior.
People are reaching out for an antidote against unwar-
ranted guilt feelings, needless shame, and lack of self-
worth, all heaped on them as children—a guilt trip, as
they call it. Intense feelings of guilt can make life unbearable.

Not all these negative feelings can be laid at the feet

of our elders, of course. We do some of it to ourselves. Often there's no discernible reason. It just exists within us. We can hardly expect to avoid all unneccessary feelings of guilt, but we can help ourselves with two basic questions when we are getting caught on the wrong track: "Why do I feel guilty?" and "Should I feel guilty?" You may not always get an honest answer or a deep insight. But you'll raise an important doubt, which can, in turn, help you avoid having to make unreasonable demands on yourself.

AGING

One way to look at getting older is to say, "Whatever age I am is the *best* age." To that I'd add, "The age we *live in* is the best age."

Although scientists may someday figure out how to extend the life span of our genes, who knows if that will be so wonderful. At which age would you like to halt the advancing years? I couldn't choose. Could you? So if you look at all the assembled data on the decline of the human body, you'll come to the inevitable conclusion that you are, if not in command, certainly in charge of supervising *how* you age. What goes on with your body is to some degree related to what goes *in*.

Sound. Be kind to your ears. They're in close proximity to your brain—and that, in turn, controls the rest of you.

Oxygen. As we get older, whether we've been active or sedentary, we should realize that our lungs don't function the way they once did. At thirty we take in twice as much air as we can at seventy. So in order to

get sufficient oxygen into your blood and brain, *exercise!*
You can use a secondhand bike, put it on a special stand,
and pedal yourself—safely—to good health. It's great
for your heart, lungs, muscles, posture, weight, and cir-
culation.

Food. As to your diet, *so much* is written and so much
is still guesswork. Let's just say that moderation and
balance are the key. You don't need extra vitamins if
you eat enough fruits and vegetables.

Tobacco. Tobacco ages your lungs by more than a
decade, just as sun ages your skin.

Above all, our *own attitude* about aging remains essential.

ANGER

It was the opinion of George Jean Nathan, the drama
critic, that "no man can think clearly when his fists are
clenched." Thus he defined anger—no doubt in the
days before his consciousness was elevated to include
women.

I've been seeing quite a bit of publicity about anger.
Controversy is raging: Is it good to vent it? Beneficial to
release it? Can it be constructive, physically and emotionally? Or do we harm ourselves and those around us
when we explode our grievances, shrapnel fashion? As
with almost everything else, the pendulum is swinging
once again. "Letting it all hang out" may not do any
good, after all. An angry mood is much too easy to
sustain—for some, indefinitely. Listen to conversations
around you in public places and you will make the
startling observation that nine out of ten seem to deal

with complaints about something, someone, or "them" —whoever or whatever that may be.

Does internalizing feelings of anger cause ulcers? Heart attacks? Headaches? Will it make you anorexic or obese? For a time, psychiatrists believed that we should release anger, for our own good. Now they're not so sure it serves a useful purpose. Dr. Carol Tavris, who wrote a book on the subject, suggests that "talking out an emotion doesn't reduce it; it rehearses it." Isn't that what people are doing when they rail against the boss or co-worker in the washroom and against their roommate or spouse at lunch. When we think of being "livid," we forget that it means pale, drained of blood— not hot-headed. What we lose when we lose our temper is the blood supply to the brain, which impairs our thinking process.

So George Jean Nathan was right! Fury is a storm that blows out your mind.

FEAR OF FREE TIME

One of the less recognizable symptoms of retirement is apprehensiveness. Believe it or not, an overabundance of leisure can present as much of a problem as overwork and too many responsibilities. "Fear of free time" prevents some people from even considering retirement. For others, it ruins their newfound freedom, especially if they had no choice in the timing.

The level of energy and self-imposed productiveness standards must now be modified and rechanneled. The weariness that we might feel at the moment of occupational cutoff doesn't actually last very long. A few weeks of rest and relaxation will wash away exhaustion. To feel refreshed and ready for the next plateau, there must be some genuine eagerness to get there—a plan, a reason, a goal, a commitment.

Perhaps you know someone who feels burned out and may well be perpetuating this weariness—unconsciously—because there's nothing to go on to. Enthusiasm, productiveness, stimulating activities, intellectual progress—these are the ingredients for avoiding an enervating retirement routine. When you first come out of the work-weary fog and clear the air around you, begin by developing a new level of awareness for your surroundings; you'll be amazed at what you've been missing. Now that you're less involved with work, you have time to become more responsive—first to yourself, then to your mate and to the world. I wonder if I speak for almost everyone when I suggest, now that you've stopped *work,* that you might want to learn to *play.* "Nose to the grindstone" ethics, which dominated our upbringing, have prevented many from developing into playful, uninhibited adults.

If you find you can only play when there's a child around, you have a good reason to relearn. Now is the best time.

LEARNING TO TEACH

Most Americans go to school for at least twelve to sixteen years; many for twenty to twenty-two years. How much time do you suppose we spend learning how to *teach?* Probably none, unless we're training to become educators. But isn't that what we all *are* some of the time—teachers? Your first job is baby-sitting, the next one, camp counselor; you're already teaching!

As parents, that's what we do every day—instruct, inform, educate, guide. Husbands and wives try to school each other, too, on subjects with which one is more familiar than the other. They say *he* should never try to teach *her* to drive a car. Well, maybe the problem is with the method, not the master. Any job we ever hold has to do with being instructed or instructing someone else. Taking direction is a never-ending thing in the theater. It must be given *and* accepted with mutual respect.

Much of what we learn in school is for training the mind to absorb, retain, and recall information. We're taught how to study. We don't learn how to teach—and that's the serious lack. Tension in our daily lives frequently stems from the way we communicate information to each other. It's seldom done effectively. Either it creates antagonism or is inadequately transmitted and, therefore, useless.

A friend told me that as a volunteer teacher's aide in a remedial reading program, she had the great fortune to be working with an inspired teacher. She learned *so much* about how to teach. She only regretted not having had that ability when she was a young mother herself, when she could have applied the *positive* approach to the education of her own children.

LONELINESS

How do *you* handle loneliness? Apparently we all have two things in common when it comes to feeling lonely and forlorn: we don't know how to talk about it, *and* we usually are a little ashamed. Somehow we get the notion that we aren't supposed to feel that it's our own fault.

Anyone can feel uncomfortably alone or deserted—it has little to do with age, family, or social position. You can be married, have loving children, a nice circle of friends—and still experience "sounds of silence." There are days when an unexplained sense of abandonment overtakes us. To whom can we talk about it? Sometimes no one. To speak of it to your spouse may give the impression of dissatisfaction and petulance. If we say it to our children, we may appear to be demanding and possessive. If we admit it to our friends, we make them feel inadequate or uncaring. Should we speak of it at all? *Yes,* but it's not easy.

Mere consolation is usually ineffective or inappropriate; advice, patronizing. It doesn't help to be told "everyone feels that way." When one feels lonely, there's little comfort in well-intentioned advice to keep yourself busy, join a club, take a course, get a job, make new friends. Coming home to an empty house is unbearable to most people. It *is* a condition of life—for some schoolchildren, the divorced, the widowed.

Loneliness can become an illness if dwelled on unnaturally or compensated for with liquor or drugs or overeating. But it can be easier to cope with if recognized as a normal, common occurrence, which is usually temporary. Therapy can help if the feeling of despair is chronic and self-criticism accompanies hopelessness. *Being alone* is not to be equated with loneliness, any more than being with people is a guarantee against it. Recognize it for what it is—inevitable! Don't let it get the better of you for long.

Nothing is forever—not marriage, not family, not

friends. Newly formed companionship can be more meaningful if we don't try to think of it in terms of a lifetime. The only thing we really can control is how we spend our time. Chasing rainbows is a bit too fanciful for any time of your life.

LOVE OF LEARNING

With all the renewed furor about educational shortcomings, it might pay to look at our *motivations* for learning. We tell children they must learn in order to do well—to succeed, in the economic sense, of course. We fill magazines and newspapers with exposés and editorials which warn that the Russians and Japanese are going ahead, at full steam, on megapower, while we're idling. Educators collect academic degrees in order to ensure seniority. In other professions, people go for a masters or doctorate because their *positions* would otherwise be in jeopardy. But what about the love of learning? If school isn't *fun*, from the beginning—and all the way through—we miss the point of what an education really is.

Meg Greenfield of *Newsweek* magazine explains her feelings about educational aims: "The activity, itself, pursued not just in school, but rather, throughout a lifetime, *is* the payoff." I agree with her that we must create a "learning society—one devoted to the joys and rewards of continuous learning, as distinct from the one-shot passing of some exam."

Here I am, eighty-three years old, and I have just returned from yet another travel of discovery to the Greek Islands. And I couldn't pass up a quick side trip to see the Monet Gardens in France. For what? For my own love of discovery, of learning, of being a student.

When an orthodox Jewish child is brought to the ancient Talmud for his first lesson—at the age of four or five—a bit of honey is placed on the book for him to taste—to taste the sweetness of knowledge. German children are given a large, colorful paper sack of candy to take to their first day in class. These are not rewards, but *promises.*

OLD AGE IN RUSSIA

Stories have been coming from remote regions of Russia about the unusual longevity of some of their men and women. Not only do these people get to be very old, they remain vigorous and continue to work, think, and play into their tenth decade and beyond.

To live a long time *and* be productive is everyone's dream—not just in the mountain village of Abkhazia, near the Black Sea. Apparently, to enjoy *good* old days is closely associated with how you treat yourself and how you are treated. Specialists who sit around discussing these matters in symposiums come to just those obvious conclusions. (I'm sure they were obvious, long ago, to my grandmother!)

That Russian region boasts five times as many centenarians as we can produce here. The village of Abkhazia is presided over by its elders. In this society, a "gerontocracy," old villagers participate in the council of elders and perform hospitality roles which are an important part of local custom. Younger citizens rely on them for guidance and advice. The benefits are twofold: their culture, knowledge, and experience are passed on, and they attain the status they deserve—*reverence*. They retain their self-image by continuing their influence on household and community. In other words, they aren't set aside.

We, on the other hand, have not yet learned to perpetuate our all-American talent for self-sufficiency and feelings of self-worth into the later years. It's precisely this loss which makes us more likely to become frail, depressed, and susceptible to illnesses associated with aging. So far, no real genetic differences have been found between us and these people in Russia. Yogurt alone can't be the reason. I think what *we* need is better public relations.

PACE

Those who may best understand the difficulties of the elderly are not necessarily professional counselors with a string of degrees after their names. *Peer counseling* is being introduced in Santa Ana, California. It is called Psychological Alternative Counseling for Elders—PACE, for short.

Two licensed social workers train volunteers in a nine-week course and then conduct seminars, in which cases are discussed. The course trains volunteers to recognize problems, offer crisis intervention, and refer clients to professionals when necessary. So far, there are twenty-eight older volunteers who counsel their fellow seniors on how to cope with problems of aging.

I wouldn't be surprised if a good part of the success of PACE is attributable to the fact that *someone else cares*.

Perhaps caring isn't just an emotion but a science, like mathematics, because it appears that when we divide it, it somehow seems to multiply.

I'm sure we've all had the experience when trying to help an older person with advice or emotional support —a kind of angry rebuff came our way. Such negative response is usually based on the attitude that "if you're not in this boat, you can't know how overwhelming the waves look."

Christopher Hayes, director of Santa Ana's PACE, came upon his peer-group-support idea while working his way through college as an orderly in a nursing home. Because he knows many seniors cannot or will not seek help, he sends his mobile unit to senior centers, nutrition sites, and homes. PACE workers include retired nurses, businesspeople, and teachers. Most are trying to cope with the beginning problems of their own aging. This, then, helps the volunteer see his or her future and, perhaps, rethink and reconstruct his life.

We're all in this together. So I'm glad we're beginning to reach out to each other.

PERSONAL PROBLEMS?

Quilting bees and stove-side chats were the tried and trusted American ways of raising consciousness before the days of psychotherapy, encounter groups, and Alcoholics Anonymous. All of us, without exception, think of our problem as *unique*. The bigger the problem, the more unique we think it is. If we talk to friends or relatives about it, one of two things happens: either the sympathetic listener will try to cheer us up by suggesting "it isn't as bad as all that," or the reaction will be somewhat competitive and we'll have to hear how really bad it is with *him*. One-upmanship at its worst!

What we discover when we join a group—*organized troubleshooting*—is that we *share* many of the same dilemmas. We come to the realization that as long as we think of what bothers us as personal problems instead of collective problems, we can make little headway in finding a solution. But collective problem solving leads to collective solutions. When we get a case of the jitters, we make ourselves ill. It's not necessary to call it hypochondria. Tension, fear, anger, apprehension—all this and many other emotions affect us physically: headaches, back pain, intestinal disturbances, even cancer!

There's some data that show that cancer patients often experienced a major loss in their family or lives six months before the onset of the disease. Having a "type A personality" makes us 50 percent more prone to heart problems. One hundred years ago, when life expectancy was a great deal shorter, the major causes of death and illness were infectious diseases. Now we are made ill by stress, which we attempt to minimize in a variety of unhealthy ways—alcohol, drugs, gambling, tobacco, spending sprees, overeating.

There are many support groups to help us understand and conquer these problems. We need only to acknowledge *that we are not alone*.

"PLAYFAIR"

At what point in our education to become civilized adults do we learn to inhibit our natural instinct to have *fun?* We do most of our playing in the first five years of life. It is then that the right hemisphere of the brain—the artistic/creative side—has all the fun. In school we start to work on the other side of the brain—the analytic/learning center.

Dr. Matt Weinstein says that "people are not, by nature, depressed or bored, yet everyone on this planet gets that way." He blames it all on too much work. Play is absolutely essential to stress reduction. This doctor and his Berkeley, California-based Playfair group try to combat these common problems of adulthood. They display their playful antics—their fun philosophy—before colleges, conventions, and nursing homes. Noncompetitive amusement is the course of study—not kids' games, which are usually much too goal oriented.

According to Dr. Weinstein and his "comedics," it's the stress and competition of childhood games that make most of us withdraw from playfulness. Another factor is our conscience. The Judeo-Christian work ethic, so ingrained in our upbringing, makes us feel guilty when we don't work or aren't otherwise engaged in some serious pursuit. If we overwork and underplay, we tend to feel depressed. If we overplay and underwork, we feel we're ignoring our responsibilities.

Play should be a routine part of our days. It's mandatory, not elective. One doctor, who has witnessed the benefit of laughter in cancer patients, says, "I don't laugh because I'm happy; I'm happy because I laugh."

In a recent transatlantic flight, I didn't rent the earphones because I'd already seen the film, which was a comedy. This gave me an opportunity to observe the passengers. Only one man and his wife laughed loudly, frequently, and in unison. To the happy couple!

RETIRING

Retirement has been the goal of the working classes since the beginning of the Industrial Revolution. Before that men worked until they no longer could. Women never stopped. Perhaps we should not give up that idea so quickly.

In actuality, only blue- and white-collar workers *want* to retire. The wealthy, the powerful, intellectuals, and professionals usually stay in their careers or choose a different one for later on—one which will keep them as busy and involved as ever. U.S. presidents don't seem to retire. Apparently, neither do conductors, writers, actors, scientists. What big industry accomplishes by retiring its workers is really defeating its own purpose. Inexperienced employees come in to replace capable, trained people, whose competence is then lost to industry. Workers, in turn, lose much more than they gain: free time, for what?

Retirement income is often inadequate. And because many people are shackled to a retirement fund, they can't leave their place of employment to start a new career.

Planning for your so-called retirement should not be merely a matter of finances. No scheme, no matter how ingenious, can guarantee to support you and your spouse for ten, twenty, or thirty years. Plan to *retool*, not retire; choose a path which will lead to an occupation—part- or full-time—mentally, physically, and financially suited to your needs. Teaching, I think, should be one of the avenues open to maturians—using what we have spent a lifetime acquiring, to broaden the experiences of the young.

So, if you're looking to invest in your future, do it by investing in your mind. Life begins at retirement—not because your job is finally behind you but because the world is suddenly opening up before you, and you've prepared yourself for your debut.

SCOUTING

Look at the world, now and then, through young eyes. Any adult, no matter which birthday you've passed, can see things in a new light by a very simple device: take a small hand in yours and go out looking. Have you taken a child to a museum lately? Taken a walk in the woods with a youngster? Gone to explore another part of town, in the company of a couple of kids?

Well, perhaps you haven't got children readily available to help you rediscover the world. Let me suggest that Girls Scouts—and Boy Scouts—welcome participation by mature members of our society, both men and women. You have so much to offer, and those kids pay you back with generous grins, golden giggles, and wide-eyed wonder. Whether your interests are in the realm of mushrooming or photography, finance or medicine, there are scout troops who'll appreciate your participation.

Senior participation in scouting is nothing new. There are over 500,000 of us involved right now, with the Girls Scouts alone! Such involvement by mature adults is an integral part of their organization. The volunteer experience touches each in a personal manner. For us, it's an opportunity to interact with young people; for the young, it's a chance to be with an adult who is neither parent nor teacher. It can also provide a worthwhile retirement career opportunity (for husband and wife as a team, even!), making use of knowledge acquired through work and in life.

Sir Robert Baden-Powell, founder of the Boy Scout movement, said to "look wide." To that I'd like to add: look *close* and relearn the child's-eye view.

STRESS

They say stress is a killer. But I think no stress is equally deadly, especially as you get older. If your days just seem to slip by without any highs and lows, without some anxieties and pulse-quickening occurrences, you may not be *really living*. Stress, if it's not extreme, is stimulating. It's especially good for you if you either manage to resolve the cause or learn to adapt.

Trying to avoid all possibly stressful situations is unrealistic. We can't be creative without stress. Satisfaction comes from accomplishment—and that's only gratifying if it was a challenge. But what can you do to counteract the kind of stress that may be too much for you? Too often? Insoluble? Learn to ride with it, if you can. If not, find your own form of healthful release.

The first thing you must learn about relieving stress is not to turn to chemical solutions. Pills and alcohol only tend to aggravate the situation. Every time you come down from that cloud, you hit an air pocket with a thud. Instead, prepare now for the next stress time. Think about the things you really like to do—activities that get you "out of yourself" and make you forget what's bothering you.

Do something that pleases you. Shopping is great, but only if you can afford it and it won't add feelings of guilt to the already existing tensions. Pleasing or pampering *someone else* is even better for you. Spend some time with an amusing friend or see a funny film. Just as humans can create unreasonable stress, so too only humans can laugh. Exercise, especially outdoors, so that nature becomes the environment.

And don't feel guilty about sweeping the whole mess out the front door—it's better than sweeping it under the carpet. Because *there* it will trip you up later.

SYMPTOMS

The American Heart Association occasionally runs a series of public service announcements regarding high blood pressure. Apparently it's a disease with no discernible symptoms. That means many people who have this ailment *don't know it.*

One study shows that among those who *know* they have high blood pressure, 90 percent think they can *feel* symptoms, such as headaches, nervous tension, flushed faces, and fast heartbeat. There are good reasons why it's difficult for people to believe in an ailment without a detectable symptom—and why they will *insist* on feeling such symptoms anyhow. As children, when we had fever, pain, and sore throats (due to flu or measles), we became conditioned to associate symptoms with ill health.

We all should try not to think so often about the possibility of illness. We automatically say, "I hope you're not catching cold" when someone sneezes. A routine visit to the doctor makes us search our bodies for symptoms. He's bound to ask how we *feel*. So we tend to make ourselves feel worse, because we think it's expected of us. Not all illnesses have symptoms, however. High blood pressure is just one of them.

So, take it to heart! Concentrate more on what you eat; it is true that we *are* what we eat. Why do people find it so difficult to believe that foods affect mental and physical well-being, when almost everyone is willing to concede that there are food allergies and that chemicals in the form of medications can help—or hurt—us.

DR. RUTH WESTHEIMER

Recently Cornell University Northshore Hospital, on Long Island, New York, held a day-long seminar called A Positive Approach to Senior Years. Participants were citizens and medical professionals. Among the speakers was Dr. Ruth Westheimer: lecturer, educator, consultant. Her subject was human sexuality.

On this day she addressed herself to senior sexuality. As she says, if someone had told her when she was a student at the Sorbonne that she would someday talk openly over the airwaves about sex, she would have thought it a feeble joke. After all, we come from an age when these things were not discussed. We *had* no words with which to discuss it. We played with the infant and said, "Show me your eyes, your mouth, your chin, your belly button, your knee." Between the belly button and the knee there was, apparently, nothing.

When Ruth Westheimer speaks to an audience of the elderly, there are giggles, embarrassed guffaws, rueful laughter, and nods of recognition. But mostly there's a grin on everyone's face. This subject, sex—and especially senior sex—which engenders hundreds of callous jokes, is a subject that too many of these people never giggle, laugh, or smile about when they are with each other, alone. We grow old and we think we're no longer lovable. Why? Because our skin doesn't fit as well, or the bounce is gone? Nonsense.

You are lovable if:

> you like yourself,
> you like the other person,
> you maintain a happy disposition, and
> you are exciting.

Do we act like a dirty old man or, worse, a dirty old woman, if we want love—and sex? I abhor those labels.

What's respectable for the young is not decadence in the old. The only obstacles to love are those you invent yourself.

TENSION

If you visit the doctor every four or six months with some undefinable complaint, it might be a good idea to keep a diary for a while. If the doctor rarely "names" your ailment and only prescribes some mild medication and more rest, chances are there wasn't much wrong with you that a lot less tension couldn't cure.

I can tell you from personal experience that stage fright is no different from school stomachache. It *is* a pain. Tension, whether brought on by real or imagined problems, can do the darnedest things to your body. Headaches, of course, are a common result, as is indigestion. But it's also possible to have chest pains, say, on the right side, or dizziness. Impaired vision, leg cramps, even an earache or a toothache often can be traced to tension. Wait a few weeks before you think about getting new glasses or having your teeth X-rayed.

Try to swim with the tide, so to speak, instead of brooding about the events in your life or the world. If you're sleeping restlessly, for example, you may be grinding your teeth, which will certainly make them sensitive and can even cause earaches. You might need a bite plate and a lighter meal before bedtime instead of tests, drugs, or dentistry.

Your diary will tell you a great deal when you look back at the weeks preceding the visit to the doctor. All too often you were a "bundle of nerves"—and that *is* painful. Now don't misunderstand me: I don't advocate that *you* diagnose your own symptoms *all the time.* Just have a good look at how tightly wound you are before you ask for professional help.

You and your body will get along better if you take on some of the responsibility yourself.

MEMORY RETRIEVAL

Many of us confuse "remembering" with "retrieving." We may take it as a sign of aging when our memory doesn't perform to expectation, but there is no scientific evidence to think so—only myths and bugaboos which have a way of feeding on themselves.

What makes us stutter while trying to introduce someone we've known for years and, suddenly, we draw a blank? Nervousness, tension, shyness, impatience with ourselves. We didn't really *forget* the name; we just have trouble retrieving it at a moment's notice. We become ashamed or fearful, which aggravates the situation.

Older people can remember as well as ever; it just may take a little more patience and organization. It isn't true that memory fades after fifty or sixty. We are simply less interested in the minor aspects of daily life. We block them out. We may also be less motivated to remember, and so let our brains get lazy. *Exercise that muscle* and, like any other, it will continue to serve you!

Fewer than one sixth of all elderly persons suffer from any kind of brain damage that might impair memory or other intellectual function. If I misplace my date book, perhaps it's my subconscious playing hide and seek, because I'm engaged in entirely too many activities! What *does* change as we get older? Not intellectual capacity, but only the swiftness with which we can process new information and retrieve stored knowledge. We walk a little slower, too, and that doesn't embarrass us. Therefore, we shouldn't get bent all out of shape when thought processes take a little more time. Relax and acquire a few little tricks:

Pay closer attention.
Try to concentrate on one thing at a time.
Link what you want to remember to a strong
visual image.
Use a calendar not just for birthdays and
appointments but for lists of other
information, too.

Above all, try to relax and *take your time*. Even a youngster can't remember his address when he's lost or frightened.

A WEIGHTY PROBLEM

Some people have all the luck! A lady from Sarasota, Florida, complained to me that all she hears and reads is how to lose weight. Until recently she was still the same 102 pounds she weighed when she got married—sixty-five years ago! In the last two years she lost 10 pounds, and though her doctor tells her she is just fine, she worries about it. She may be unaware that it's much healthier to weigh less as we get older because our bodies require smaller quantities of food. I don't know how tall she is, so I'm not sure 90 pounds is too thin. But if she really wants to gain, that same little calorie counting booklet used by the overweight can help her choose foods that put on weight.

After a certain age, energy requirements diminish. If we eat more than we need, we only strain the system unnecessarily. Right amounts of food increase our resistance to disease and raise the level of vitality, enhancing our well-being. Exercise helps the body burn off excess calories, but it can also stimulate the need for food. The lady from Sarasota who wishes to gain weight may have become a bit too sedentary to work up a good appetite.

We are admonished to eat a balanced diet, a variety of foods. In one lifetime each of us eats more than sixteen ten-ton trucks of food—but was it all nutritious? Not if most of it was processed on the assembly line. We will not necessarily develop ill health or malnutrition just because we fail to consume a magic number of daily RDAs (Recommended Dietary Allowances). Natural and fresh is what counts.

We have at our disposal the most astounding variety of good food. All we need do is make sensible selections and combinations, present it attractively, and eat it under pleasant circumstances.

CONSPIRACIES

"Your plane leaves from Gate 23B," says the clerk with a smile as she hands back my validated ticket. It never fails! It's always the last gate! I have a suspicion that the first dozen or so gates are props; no plane I've ever been on left from Gate 2.

We can get the feeling that the world is constantly against us. Whose plumber comes at 8 in the morning? Not mine. Nor is he still at home when his grouchy wife grunts "he's gone" at 7:30 A.M. The oil pan leaks the day after the auto mechanic has fixed the transmission. Where was he looking while my car was up on the lift?

Deliveries to my house seem to be scheduled with an apparent antipathy to me. While side streets are choked with trucks from early morning on—Parcel Post, department stores, United Parcel, General Electric, Telephone Company, Sears—no delivery ever arrives at *my* door before 5:30 P.M. I'm the last stop of the day—regardless of any promise made by the trucking company.

Who gets the new carpet installed at 9 A.M.? And completed the same day?

Do air conditioners ever arrive before lunch? And get hooked up?

Medical appointments are another one of those conspiracies. Call the nurse thirty minutes before the scheduled time—to make sure the doctor is not still in the operating room or stacked up over Boston. She confirms your appointment and says, "Yes, please be on time."

You walk in and see twenty people turning pages in outdated magazines without reading a word. There must be three doctors back there, you hope; but oh, you know you're dreaming. A one-hour wait is just enough time to rehearse your ailment—four or five times—in fine detail.

When you have an important engagement, the dress you plan to wear either isn't back from the cleaners, was never sent there, or has a zapped zipper.

If all your days go something like this, isn't it funny that mine do, too? Perhaps we are not the target, you and I. Apparently everyone is.

WORK OUT

A young architect could make a good beginning in his career with a design for small hospitals at the base of a ski lift. Osteopaths on the way to success should locate near a good-sized tennis complex.

The sporting goods store in town is called Sweats. Sports have taken the place of physically exhausting labor. Machines have robbed us of the chance to build our bodies. To keep the billions of cells fired up, we don't work—we work out. The woven rattan carpet beater has not been swung against the old Oriental rug hung over an iron bar in the backyard since grandmother put it down sixty years ago. It's lovingly displayed on the wall, a treasured antique, looking just like a tennis racket! Perhaps as many as 70 percent of runners sustain an injury every year. Walking to the store or, heaven forbid, walking to school never caused such bodily devastation. Certainly none that *I* can remember.

Top-of-the-line training shoes (formerly called sneakers) can cost as much as $100 and weigh a remarkably few ounces—heel stabilizers, bouncy thick soles, and arch-support system included. But that's not good enough. Five-pound weights are strapped to each ankle to increase the benefits of running or walking. Runners are also clutching hand weights—two to five pounds apiece—which sell like mittens in January to folks with flabby arms, weak hands, and limp wrists.

The world's most efficient human-power machine, the bicycle, no longer takes you anywhere; it's imprisoned in the cellar, together with a rowing machine and the TV at eye level, so the pleasure of stationary motion can be tempered with the day's bad news. These gleaming chrome muscle builders help sedentary citizens achieve the same benefits formerly derived from digging, climbing, carrying, scrubbing, weeding, planting, cutting, sawing, shoveling, hammering, plowing, baling, grinding.

No longer are there mailboxes down the street. They've been redesigned for drive-by drop-offs along Main Street. The verb "to go" has lost its "get up."

SEX AFTER SIXTY

A pioneer in gerontology, Dr. Robert Butler, stated that physicians who graduated from medical school prior to 1961 had no formal instruction in sex education. Certainly no one taught them anything about "sex after sixty." Sheer ignorance has long been to blame for lack of interest among older persons, which results in depression and ill health.

For women, menopause or even a hysterectomy should not influence their sensuality or sex life. Signs of age become insurmountable blocks only in the mind. There's *no* proven link between old age and the decline of sexual desire. Are we still in the Dark Ages about our midsections? Apparently yes, if you look into most of the research literature available until quite recently. Even well-known studies (Kinsey, Masters and Johnson, etc.) seem to drop off at the edge of the world when they get to the magic number: sixty.

Older people who pretend not to want physical gratification, or reject such intimacy, usually share two other thoughts: that they are no longer attractive, and that people would think it shameful. At the very time in life when loving should be most enjoyable, least encumbering, we give it up! For life to endure, love must endure. But we haven't always been taught that. Physical reactions *do* change when we get older. In many cases that is taken as a signal that the sexual response has ended. We retain our youthful images of sex, as well as the early training that unconsciously prepares us for total denial as soon as *perfectly normal* changes occur. Instead of learning to make adjustments, we establish avoidance patterns.

Consciousness raising, in private groups or through the media, was used successfully some years ago for improving awareness of human equality. And I think it's the logical approach for educating the public about sex after sixty.

MAXIMUM LIFE SPAN

Have you noticed that trademark characters are on a diet-and-fitness program? Betty Crocker's features are now less round. The White Rock girl, poised as ever for a swim, has lost weight—on lo-cal soda, I presume. Even the cherubic Campbell kids, though still dimple-kneed and apple-cheeked, look slimmer in their britches and are wearing skates. Fit is fashionable. Pudgy is passé. We're shaping up. Scarlett's corset is not a big seller, and Auntie Mame is trying to look less ample.

The gerontologist Dr. Roy Walford wrote a book

called *Maximum Life Span,* in which he gives his own dietary and exercise program for living to 120 years and more—he hopes. He quotes the 78-year-old Professor Thomas Cureton (I like that name), the so-called father of physical fitness: "Without daily aerobic exercise of 30 minutes, women reach their peak of fitness at 14, men at 17."

Exercise is also said to increase the oxidation capacity of the brain and to improve its information-processing capability. According to Dr. Walford, aerobic—not static—exercise "adapts the body to *taking in, transporting* and *using* oxygen at an increased rate." In his book he elaborates on his theory of caloric undernutrition—not malnutrition, of course—the benefits of eating foods high in nutrients and low in calories. He points out that weight reduction without physical exercise is unwise and "can cause loss of bodily power." How product logo characters get thinner is difficult to figure out when you read what Dr. Walford has to say about factory-processed foods—what he calls "naked calories." For instance, 22 to 32 percent of the weight of many boxed cereals is *added* honey or sugar. Each of us puts away about (oh, this is terrible!) 128 pounds of sugar each year. A 12-ounce can of Coca-Cola—the most American contribution to the world's food supply —contains *nine* teaspoons of sugar.

The image which food fabricators want to project should start in their laboratory, not in the art department.

Part 3

Why endeavor to straighten
the road of life?
The faster we travel, the less
there is to see.

WRITTEN MEMORIES IN THE ATTIC

Those of us who've had the task of liquidating the dwelling and possessions of a relative—a parent, perhaps—have had the ultimate look into someone's life. It usually includes searching through cartons and containers and finding notes, letters, diaries, pictures, and mementos: tangible evidence that here lived a person who cared, loved, hoped, fretted, wanted to be remembered and to remember.

Did your parents save their love letters? Were there comic comments under the faded sepia photographs pasted on black album pages? What a lot of fun they had making their own entertainment: Isadora Duncan poses. Costume parties aboard ship or picnics by an unidentified lake. Baby books, in which each new ounce, word, food, or talent was lovingly recorded.

How is it today? We keep photos, yes; even recordings, videotapes, and home movies. But not much is *written down;* no observations are recorded on paper. Phone calls bring news, questions, problems. But we don't write. Do people still keep a record of what children say? And comment on it?

Future generations will have less memorabilia to sort through, I'm sure. This is the age of the technological takeover—and it does have its advantages! I watched the face of a first-time soon-to-be-grandmother, whose pregnant daughter was showing sonograms of her five-month fetus. This young woman, a pediatric surgeon, showed us these unintelligible, cosmic-looking photos. But then she added her own outline drawings of the baby on tracing paper to help us "read" the sonograms. One of these overlays identified the arm bent up toward the head, four fingers over the face, and the thumb in the mouth. "Don't I have a genius there!" she bragged. She had not yet felt the baby move. But she had *watched* it move on the screen.

No box in the attic ever offered up such a surprise before. The techno-treasures of the future! Sound writings!

WORKING DAUGHTERS

The new women aren't members of the leisure class, regardless of age, financial or social position. At one and the same time, they *are* and *are not* "just" wives, "only" mothers, "merely" daughters. Working women now outnumber those who don't work outside the home. A young mother, who had been a full-time schoolteacher before her children were born, told me she wasn't "doing anything now."

I think perhaps we've made our young women too aware of their options—to the point where they feel unnerved. Although it *is* work to be a mother, the career woman has all kinds of additional stresses. One that she may not have counted on was her role as daughter. In former times the middle-aged housewife was just about getting free of her own family duties when her aging parents became more and more dependent on her. That worked out fairly well then. Now, however, the traditional bearer of this burden is already over-loaded.

The working woman who contributes to her family status or, in many cases, is sole support of herself and her children, is hard pressed when a parent becomes an additional dependent. At first it's just a question of help with paperwork, decision making, or visits to the doctor. Soon it leads to a combined living arrangement. This is not only an emotional strain; often time, space, and money are in as short supply as tact and temper.

In this short space I can give only a few words of advice: we *must* practice "consciousness raising." Talking out loud, in public, about these problems will focus national attention and awareness on them.

A few years ago women all over the world found out that their sisters everywhere all had pretty much the same problems in their private lives; solutions were found, little by little, through recognition. We must let each other know how prevalent this situation is—that "you are not alone."

HELEN HAYES THEATRE, AGAIN

It has been said that an actress is someone who makes faces for a living. Well, to some extent, certainly. It works effectively in motion pictures, television, *and* the stage—*if* the audience doesn't number in the thousands. You can't see a glint in the eye, a turned-down mouth, or a raised eyebrow if you're sitting in as huge a theater as Mr. Portman is building over what was once the Helen Hayes Theatre, west of Broadway.

Acting is an interpretive art. *Who* is on the stage

makes a difference. If you can't see the facial expressions, the move of a muscle, or hear the subtle nuances of the voice—without amplification!—you might as well save the forty dollars, buy the book, and read it yourself. Thank goodness I'm not alone in this opinion. The folks who own the Little Theatre know how I feel and they have renamed their lovely playhouse on Forty-fourth Street after me.

Built in 1912 by my friend producer Winthrop Ames, the Little Theatre has metamorphosed several times—from theater to conference center and concert hall, to TV studio, and back again to legitimate theater. Even its name has seesawed back and forth a couple of times, and I just hope that we two will now stay as one. Winthrop Ames built his Little Theatre for the production of small, intimate drama that could not survive in the commercial atmosphere of Broadway. Originally it seated only 299 persons. The opening production was (appropriately, it seems to me) *The Pigeon*, by John Galsworthy. It now seats almost 500 theatergoers—each one of whom will have the opportunity to establish direct contact with the actors and actresses on the stage.

The present owners of the Helen Hayes Theatre, Mr. Markinson and Mr. Tick, insurers of theaters, were dismayed to see the demolition of the small and beautiful playhouses in New York and determined to save as many as they could. This is their first purchase. God bless them!

ZANESVILLE, U.S.A.

In spite of the billion-dollar "instant music business," I was heartened to learn that there still are people who enjoy *making music* and singing. You might be interested to read what folks in Zanesville, Ohio, do. (I love that town's name! A place for *zany* self-entertainment.) This is what Helen Conrath wrote to me:

There's an old-time riverboat here, the *Lorena Sternwheeler,* that makes Wednesday evening trips, from May to October—with dinner and entertainment by The Touring Company. Sixty-nine-year-old Hazel Russi plays the organ in that unique old style, which provides a background for the lovely trip up the lazy Muskingum River. Don Mathes and I help serve dinner, tell the story of the boat and the sights, along the way. When the sun has started to set, the little boat heads back to Zanesville. It is then that the mood begins to change to nostalgia, and we three take over with a show that delights the audience.

We entertain with music from every decade, show tunes and even Archie Bunker's "Those Were The Days." By the time The Touring Company has completed its *George M* medley, *everyone* is singing. Song sheets are handed out and, believe it or not, *everyone*, young and old, sings all the way home. Even Captain Nelson Brown, a retired riverboat pilot with fiery red hair, solos with "When Irish Eyes Are Smiling." It's exciting to hear a boatload of 100 people singing "God Bless America" at the top of their lungs, floating down the river!

There are lots of hugs and kisses, and friendly handshakes, as the guests depart—and the friendship and warmth of the evening lingers on for a long time. People from all over the country have visited our little boat and enjoyed a cruise down the river with us. When they say, "It was the most enjoyable time I've had all year," we believe it.

Well, so do I, Zanesville! I will tell a captain I know who cruises the Hudson River about it. We sure can use some of that spontaneity.

LEVERAGE IN THE MATURIAN VOTING BOOTH

Do you remember the first time you voted? In those days we weren't considered mature enough to form opinions on such weighty matters—by whom and how we were to be governed—until we reached the magic number twenty-one. Eighteen-year-olds were eligible to toss hand grenades in battle, but *not* to cast ballots!

I'm glad all that has changed. But I really wonder: *do* eighteen-year-olds vote? Older people certainly do. Gray power is expected to play an ever-increasing role in American politics. Declining birth rate and advancing longevity—the seesaw is tipping to our side.

An older electorate is better informed, more experienced. Today's candidates are sensitive to the voting strength of maturians. One out of nine voters is now over sixty-five. Many are first- or second-generation Americans to whom voting is a privilege; they cast a larger percentage of the vote than their numbers would indicate.

In the 1980 presidential election, 65 percent of older citizens voted, compared to only 36 percent of the eighteen-to-twenty age group. The concerns of the older voters go beyond their own welfare, beyond the current tendency to reduce governmental services and benefits, beyond temporary stopgap legislations. They care about the rest of the world, about their progeny, about the health of the planet. Gray power in the voting booth is formidable, *if* it is predicated on continuing involvement by an informed constituency.

Regional races are as important as national elections. This may be just the time and place for some of you to start a new career—in local politics. Quite often involvement in committees, even as a volunteer, can lead to a post in town government. And that's what this country is all about—grass roots.

FIVE SENSES

When Shakespeare wrote about the problems of aging, he made much of the inevitable diminishing of the senses—sight, smell, sound, taste, and touch. But before we decide to blame it all on the weakness of our bodies, consider that a lot of it is being done *for* us—or should I say *against* us.

There are sounds that you no longer can hear, *because they don't exist,* like the peaceful whir of a lawnmower, *manually* pushed on a July evening. Even the buzz of summer flies has been pretty well extermi-nated. I personally don't like the robot sounds of com-puterized cash registers. The old bell on the cash drawer had a more profitable ring to it. Food processors have taken over the grating of carrots and the chopping of parsley on a board. Few kitchens sound like home or smell like home. Microwaves, though admittedly useful and time-saving, prepare the food so fast it doesn't have time to reach your nostrils. What still looks like that eternally tempting fruit—the shiny red apple—has been in cold storage for ages, losing all flavor. I love seeing autumn leaves blowing across a lawn. But subur-ban gardeners blow them right out of existence with earsplitting automation. Which means you also won't see the tracks of the little critters in the snow because they can't find a pile of leaves under the bushes in which to live.

But most disturbing is the "touch-not" aspect of mod-ern life; almost every product is packaged in a plastic bubble, and people are in an arm's-length, hands-off mood. By losing our sense and enjoyment of touching everyday things, we might also be losing our capacity to touch one another.

PETS AGREE WITH YOU

When the University of Pennsylvania held a confer-ence on pets and people, their findings were pretty much in keeping with what you might imagine: pets are good for you!

Although most of us would limit our attachment to kittens and puppies, there are other creatures which

can improve our well-being. Though bottlenose dol-
phins may not fit into your scheme of things, they are
said to have a beneficial effect on autistic children. For
the rest of us, the more usual cat or dog—even canary
or goldfish—can have therapeutic value.

The most obvious pleasures of owning a pet come
from sharing your home with a living creature who
doesn't require much of you, doesn't argue, and wants
only to give warmth. Small animals are usually less expensive to own. For lonely or elderly people, a pet is a
welcome companion—a reason for getting up in the
morning, going for a walk, going home, feeling needed,
and, also, protected.

Walking a dog is good exercise, as well as a link to
society. People are more likely to talk to a stranger in
the company of a pet. Even sitting alone at home is
better when there is a pet beside you. Emotional stress,
anger, or sadness can often be dispelled by stroking an
animal and feeling the calming response through your
hands.

Many families acquire a pet for their young children
to help teach them kindness, responsibility, loyalty, and
love of nature. Similar benefits can be attained by providing contact with animals for residents in nursing
homes and geriatric quarters.

A pet rekindles the spirits of people who are with-
drawn, lonely, or ill. Just let a cat sit on the lap of an
elderly person; he'll do more than purr!

PET FOOD PEEVE

Do you know what a companion animal is? No, it's not a new breed—just a new term for cats and dogs that people like to keep around the house for the fun of it.

Many older people appreciate the loyalty of these live-in friends. And some of us are even old enough to remember that originally pets were domesticated for specific purposes—to watch over the sheep, catch the mice in the barn, protect the old homestead, or be a pleasant companion by the fire or on a walk.

Remember the days *before* pet food? (That industry is only forty-five years old.) Really! Dogs and cats used to eat table scraps and butcher-shop treats, in the form of waste cuts. And they flourished! Now, when we have world food shortages, starvation, and poverty, we have a *four-billion-dollar* pet-food industry.

Food for domestic animals costs as much—if not more —than people food. It's dyed red, brown, and cream-colored—to appeal to the purchaser, not the animal. Pets are totally color-blind.

I trained the goldfish in my little pond to make a sparkling display for visitors with a sprinkling of flaked goldfish food. The .07-ounce container costs a mere $1.78—an astronomical $40 per pound!

Pet food is the only product sold that's never used by the purchaser, nor is it advertised to the ultimate consumer—the pet. Yet this fiercely competitive industry "serves" over 23 million cats and 41 million dogs, which eat more than eight billion pounds of food a year.

Not only could their appetites be stilled but the national waste disposal problem could be alleviated if they ate what is good for them: table scraps. As a matter of fact, the garbage would be further reduced by eliminating all those empty cans and paper sacks. You *can* train *your* "companion animal" to like your cooking. Remember, a cat will eat a bird and not leave much other than the feathers. So don't tell me leftover chicken isn't good for him.

THE HUDSON RIVER, MY BACKYARD

Most of the great cities of the world are located adjacent to a river or an ocean. Obviously these centers of commerce and culture developed because of the accessible route of transport—water. Now, all too often, these beautiful natural resources are the back door to those same cities—shamefully neglected, polluted, and abused.

I want to brag about the river at *my* back door—the historical and oh so beautiful Hudson. I have a picture on my desk of children swimming in a clean, clear Hudson. No, it's not an old sepia print of days gone by; it's in today's newspaper! Hurray! My river lives—with increased marine life, decreased pollution, higher oxygen level, striped bass and Atlantic sturgeon!

I am so pleased with the good news about the Hudson that I celebrated my eighty-second birthday cruising the river with my friends aboard an excursion steamer —an ex-ferryboat with the proud name of *Commander*. Because of the dual nature of my life—one half Broadway theater, with its native population and language, and the other half Nyack, a small river town with a native population and language quite different—I wanted everyone to see how clean and alive it is and how proud I am of state, local, and private efforts, which have accomplished this. The voice of the people is being heard in the land!

Soon there will be beaches and waterfront parks, marinas and fishing piers. Private housing will take the place of factories and railroad yards. Cruising the Hudson will be the perfect day-outing for citizens and visitors from all over the world.

SOMATIZERS

Interns, like any other group of young professionals, have a vocabulary all their own. You wouldn't want to hear most of their humorous or callous descriptions of patients.

A well-known acronym, for example, is GOMERs, which translates into "Get Out of My Emergency Room." It refers to the habitual clientele, the hypochondriacs, those who take advantage of free service or need human contact they can't get anywhere else. There are people who come to the emergency room in the middle of the night with a sore throat, or bring the child who has a 101-degree fever. These folks are not as sick as they *want* to be. They are looking for attention and want to make themselves important in their own eyes. We greet each other with "How are ya?" That's asking for it! Too many people feel obliged to whine a complaint in response.

A somatizer is a patient who converts emotion to

pain, and for some it's a way of life. We've all known such people. But *they* are unaware of their problem.

There are many conflicting emotions that can make us ill. If we prefer not to go to work, to school, to a party, we get a headache or intestinal upset. Pain is a way out and means someone will take care of us. But it can also be self-inflicted punishment for not doing what we know we should. Some hypochondriacs are so adept at causing and faking illness that they are actually admitted to hospitals. Perhaps as many as 40 percent of the patients seen by family doctors have no real illness. If it were only 10 percent, it would still mean twenty billion dollars spent needlessly.

Can doctors recognize these malingerers? Not easily. Their pain is real, even if the cause is imaginary. The doctor who says, "You're fine; stop worrying; come back in six months if you have any new problems," proffers an invitation to manufacture more symptoms.

Somatizers don't want to be cured and don't recognize themselves as members of this group.

VINTAGE CLOTHING SHOPS

Among the many problems the elderly face, when it's time to move into a housing development, is divesting oneself of a lifetime accumulation of belongings. Before discarding anything, do keep in mind that your new neighbors may need furniture and household items.

As for your wardrobe, the longer you've been hoarding it, the better. Your closet may play a part in starting you on a new career. If you're anything like me, you can't bear to part with the pure wool pants suit that looks like new or the beaded dress you bought for your honeymoon.

There's money on them there hangers! Vintage clothing is big business. Start collecting from friends and neighbors, and open up a shop to furnish finery to those who appreciate good workmanship, classic design, quality fabrics, as well as the wild and wonderful creations which passed like meteors, briefly, over the firmament of fashion. A vintage clothing shop located in or near a senior housing complex attracts eighteen- to thirty-five-year-old shoppers who cherish such treasures. It gives the residents a wonderful opportunity to run a *very* profitable business. Some items can be sold on consignment. Others can be bought cheaply at auctions, from other charities who don't specialize, at private sales where the value is not recognized, and through advertisements.

Preparing the merchandise for sale involves some expense, such as cleaning, and some patient hand sewing for restoration. But oh, it's a fun business, which has social and financial rewards.

CHOICES

In the 1950s and 1960s when higher education was not only more available but became a virtual necessity, some young people were what you might call professional students. They had trouble leaving school, not because they couldn't get through with it but because they couldn't get enough of it. No sooner had the young genius completed his thesis than he decided art history was not quite his bent. The law would suit him better.

Back to school, son. Back to the bank, Pop. Women's mid-century educational ambitions and career opportunities put them in the same fix.

When is higher education high enough? There are young couples today with three and four degrees between them, and I wonder whether it helps. Does it make for a more satisfactory personal life, or does it, in fact, represent framed evidence that making up your mind is more complex than training it. Agonizing over whether the chosen profession is the one which affords the best opportunities can be a roadblock to success.

The U.S. Department of Health and Human Services reports that 57 percent of all white-collar workers and 64 percent of laborers are unhappy in their jobs. Maybe they're just unhappy. Or unhappy working. We are living a transitional life. To be service-oriented is archaic. Everyone can now aspire to become . . . president of the country, the company, the club. All who occupy our living room, every day—via television—have exciting, rewarding, lucrative jobs. Ours pale by comparison.

Restlessness is the ailment to which no medical cure will ever be found. When opportunities were limited and the young were apprenticed or unquestioningly followed in their fathers' footsteps, choices were unavailable and unrealistic. It's not just in our breadwinning that we feel so footloose; our personal attachments are also open to too much questioning, too many options, too many regrets.

SPEAKING COMPUTERS

Thinking is out. Talking is in. By now we are so used to having machines verbalize to us and for us that speaking coherent sentences is unrequired and unexpected. "Like" and "ya know" take up the silent spaces formerly reserved for thinking while talking. Ask a passing salesperson, "Do you work in this department?" The answer is "No."

Not, "No, I'm sorry. You might find someone over there." That would be entirely too many words.

So what's new about that? Nothing, except that it almost startled me out of my wits when the *car* I was in said politely, "Sorry, the right rear door is ajar. Please close it." Thinking Mars had invaded, I obeyed as instructed and was rewarded with a courteous "thank you." This computerized, masterminded vehicle also speaks when car lights are on, keys are left in the ignition, fuel is running low (and the driver has his hand on the passenger's knee).

Computers can already speak. More than that, they can be engineered to listen to commands and carry out instructions. (Carry out the garbage, too, I should hope.) If your loving home computer fails to function, do you have to yell at it? Will it understand threats and promises? In West Newton, Massachusetts, the system creators are certain that soon there will be a dramatic emergence of speech recognition by computers. But which American dialect?

I know that most schools teach quite a lot about computer science; young people must be prepared for mechanization of the simplest, as well as the most intricate, phases of their lives and jobs. Speech, on the other hand, has fallen upon hard times. When every computer will have learned to recognize the sound of words and convert those to a binary vocabulary, w-o-n-t w-e a-l-l h-a-v-e t-o s-p-e-a-k t-h-e s-a-m-e?

TRAVEL

Robert Benchley once told my husband, Charlie, when they still shared bachelor quarters, that there are two kinds of travel: first-class and with children. He was young then and didn't know about the limitless pleasure of retirement travel. It can be the best, even on a budget.

The only thing you should regret about a trip is not having gone at all. New places, new foods, new faces—wherever you're going, make the most of what there is that is *different* from home. And don't compare, because that's not what you left home to do.

As for the strain of traveling, take advantage of the jet age in which you're living. Travel light, travel in comfort. The steamer trunk and the travel iron are anachronisms. The world is civilized—almost everywhere—and you *will* find aspirin, film, and shampoo, as well as a raincoat and instant coffee. Don't fret about these details, or about timetables, either. It's *never* "the last train," you know!

There are unstinting benefits available for senior citizens traveling in the United States and Canada. Did you know, for instance, that airfare discounts on Canadian carriers range from 10 percent to as much as 55 percent. A round-trip Amtrak train ticket between Los Angeles and San Francisco is under $85—and no extra charges for any stopovers you plan.

The variety in accommodations also has improved since the days when it was either hotel de luxe or motel de cay. Bed-and-breakfast accommodations are good, clean, cheap, and sociable. Rooms on college campuses can be booked between semesters. Many of the great motel chains participate in discount policies. There's a new cooperative lodging organization, through which *your* home becomes part of the chain of lodgings available to members for just a few dollars a night. Our state parks have wonderful lodges as well as campgrounds.

Benjamin Franklin thought that travel was "one way to lengthen life." If mileage counts, I'll be here forever!

SENILITY

When the aged become confused and forgetful, or incontinent and stumbling, is it due to senility, depression, or incompatible medications? A team of brain specialists has reported to the American Medical Association that "a surprisingly large number of elderly patients in nursing homes suffer from mental dementia that is potentially reversible."

There are more than one million Americans now living in nursing homes. Who knows how many could be discharged, to go back with their families, if their medical or mental condition were to be properly diagnosed and treated! Often the medication administered for a specific condition, such as a heart ailment, produces effects that can mimic senility, because the kidney may not have excreted it properly. Other times a toxic reaction to a drug, such as a tranquilizer, can cause the senility symptoms.

The aging brain becomes increasingly more susceptible to medications, and negative reactions often occur. At the same time, inadequate nutrition and dehydration can aggravate one's condition. Severe depression can also be a factor in mental dementia. Dr. Jack Rowe, a professor at Harvard Medical School, says that "if the older patient's condition is diagnosed correctly, the depression can be treated."

Unfortunately, the field of geriatric medicine is still woefully understaffed and misunderstood. Why have medical schools been dragging their feet in this department? Patients over sixty-five years old account for one fourth of hospital stays and ring up a $230 billion annual health bill. According to one medical man in this field, most doctors aren't trained in the process of aging. "Normal is often treated like disease, and disease is often ignored."

The public, as a whole, needs a new awareness *and* reassurance that much of what we think is senility is potentially reversible, with proper treatment.

VICTOR KUGLER

I once asked some nice bright young people, "Who are your heroes?" And drew a blank. "Well, not since John Kennedy," said one, and another said, "John Lennon." Real heroes, I said, someone of *today* who's doing something to be admired. "You mean death defying. Like Evel Knievel?" they asked.

I'm saddened by my minisampling of hero worship. Wasn't it great to collect clippings and pictures of your hero to put in scrapbooks? Don't you wish you still had them? We've had heroes and heroines, in peace and in war. The horror days, before the middle of this century, are imprinted in our minds. Some heroes of that time are still known to us; some, we've forgotten.

When Victor Kugler died, I realized I had forgotten his name. Kugler was the man who provided a hiding place in Amsterdam, trying to save Anne Frank and her family. *He's* a hero; his name is written in history. But who do you suppose were *his* role models? To put your life, willingly, on the line, and that of your family, isn't possible for everyone. I think one must be emulating someone. You're not *born* with the instinct to risk all for a fellow human being. To shelter this hunted group of Jews—under a Christian roof, in the face of unimaginable terror—when the whole world had closed its doors —goes far beyond the commandment to love thy neighbor.

Victor Kugler is one of my heroes. Only because Anne Frank kept a diary do we know the heroic Kugler family. If you have heroes—especially those who are *now* doing admirable things—I wish you'd write and speak about them. I have a feeling we should tell our young people who they are, so that not *all* their role models pop off the screen.

ALEXANDER GRAHAM'S BELL

On March 10, 1876, a "Bell" rang that's been making us jumpy ever since. We dash from the dinner table, drop packages as we enter the house, leap from the bathtub dripping wet. We hear it and roll out of bed, race up or down stairs, and trip over the dog. This bell was introduced into our lives by a most appropriately named gentleman from Scotland: Alexander Graham Bell.

What would we do without the telephone? Well, I have some ideas, but you'll think me old-fashioned. Unless you have a live-in secretary, the phone makes you available to the whole world—relatives who don't consider the difference in time zones, magazine salesmen who know exactly when you sit down to a meal, creditors (if you have any), or charity volunteers whose grating voices can squeeze millions out of misers.

But the telephone has many wonderful qualities, too. As a matter of fact, I have lately adopted as my most practical gift idea the remote wireless phone. What could be more convenient for a recuperating friend than a phone the size of a receiver, usable in bed, on the porch, or in the garden—in any room, in every chair! It can be a great advantage for the elderly or disabled when a cordless phone is also carried by another person (whether in the house or outside) to serve as an intercom or safety device.

Best of all, with a cordless phone we can stop jumping, running, tripping, dripping, sliding, or slamming into things . . . and we won't be tempted to resort to inelegant expletives.

OCCUPATIONAL UNISEX

The U.S. Department of Commerce has released statistics which now show an increase of men in professions that traditionally have been occupied by women. In 1960, for example, there were just over fourteen thousand male registered nurses, while in 1980 the total was close to four times as many, although the number of women nurses only doubled. But in the secretarial field, only about seven thousand more men took such a job in that twenty-year period, while an additional one and one-half million women joined the ranks.

Did you see the news item which proclaimed that the best marriages are those where both husband and wife have interests and responsibilities once considered as feminine. Oh, I can see macho types cringe and *"real"* women gasp at the thought. But it may well be true. To enjoy life and have an interest in all manner of things almost dictates that among them will be traditionally feminine pursuits. Men who reject much of what occupies a woman's mind and her time necessarily withdraw from all those activities and resort to the masculine endeavors—career, politics, sports.

The Germans came up with a phrase that separates the men from a big chunk of the real world: *Kinder, Küche, Kirche,* which means "children, kitchen, church" (in other words, "women's" concerns). In my view, those interests and their variations and side effects are the mainstay of life; men who exclude themselves are the poorer for it. As occupational stereotypes begin to fade, so will hard-and-fast "rules" of what interests a man or woman. We'll all be the beneficiaries.

THE HAPPY COUPLE

A national magazine devotes a lead article to "Private Violence," horror stories about home life. A metropolitan newspaper brings a column about married couples who find it necessary to hide their happiness. Public radio broadcasts the news that only 38 percent of our children live with both parents simultaneously, permanently. The airwaves are crackling with uncensored discussions of the most closely held aspects of private life. What's going to become of us?

In the sixties, the young tried group living to get away from what they thought couldn't work for them— the kind of bickering marriages their parents had. Why do people stay together? Dependency. And I don't think there is anything wrong with that. Isn't it what coupling is really all about? What is meant by emotional support? Why is it considered unnatural or constraining?

Good marriages are less common today. Is there something wrong with having learned to take life as it comes, making the most of the good, ignoring the rest? Marriage is not a fifty-fifty proposition. Those who make it work know it's 100 percent–100 percent. In some upper-crust ghettos (as well as the other kind), there are schoolteachers who don't have one student who lives with a mother *and* a father. No wonder the old primers need editing. The same is true with math, I suspect. Two and one don't make three. They're writing songs of love—but not about marriage. Many happily married people who do enjoy each other's company feel impelled to hide their contentment from friends and relations for fear of being deemed boring, too conventional, not contemporary. We are inundated with media psychoanalysis, forcing us to wonder what's wrong with *us*.

I appeal to all who are reasonably happily married to "show and tell" your love at every opportunity. Admit that your hot tub is just for the two of you—however unfashionable that may be considered in some circles.

SENIOR HOUSING

Stepping onto the elevator of a sparkling new senior citizen housing facility is very different from entering other high-rise transportation. You are greeted. Yes, the people who get off and on say good morning with a smile, whether they know you or not. Their territory may extend only as far as the laundry room (which, by the way, is *not* in the basement) or to the corner supermarket or the adjacent garden. But they *are* part of the community—the real world. Youngsters from neighborhood teen centers help them move in, carry their packages to the post office, run errands, hang pictures or curtains. In return they're invited to a doughnut-and-soda party. Budding gerontologists?

Gerontology has been the life's work of Dr. Robert Butler of Mount Sinai Hospital in New York City. His fellowship program is training ten to twelve thousand geriatric specialists, who will be desperately needed by the end of the decade.

A woman has just moved into a new senior housing development—soundproof ceilings, air-conditioning, triple-glazed windows. She loves nothing so much as the bright daylight and "the clean." She says, "I get up in the middle of the night and walk around the two rooms and say 'Clean! it's so clean!' "

Dr. Butler's personal imperative is to improve the lives of people who do not want to spend long years in nursing homes and who, with a little help from medicine, can live independently. More and more young interns are choosing to specialize in gerontology, a field in which not nearly enough research has been done. Passivity, the direct result of dependence on institutional living, may be responsible for many of the physical ailments besetting the elderly. Community housing is the answer—with kitchen facilities to serve meals, restaurant-style; activity rooms for entertaining and entertainment; gardens with raised flower beds for puttering.

That fosters a society that is interdependent instead of dependent.

HIRING THE RETIRING

Within the last few years we've seen a new, improved attitude about older people staying on the job. Experts on labor studies are finding a convenient correlation among three factors: the rapid increase in number of older people, the shrinking younger population, and the appearance of *robots* on the scene. They say it's a good time to be older and working.

In the opinion of Ben Fischer, one such expert, "Experience, skill, and reliability will replace muscle and endurance; even on the assembly line, robots will do the hard, physical labor, while the human worker will be a robot tender." Fischer is against forced retirement and the Social Security ruling which penalizes earnings above $5,000 a year. "We must not lure people into idleness," he says. We now have come full circle, and a lot of companies are rehiring the un-retiring.

Isn't it nice to find out that older workers are once again looked upon as a vital factor in our economy—not as millstones, but as wheels to keep things running? There's an ever-increasing shortage of younger workers, especially skilled workers. The baby boom babies of the fifties are past history, and *their* reproductive urges are not geared to halt the inversion of the population pyramid. Men and women in the executive suite are noticing great changes and are letting go of their obsession with youth.

It's just another law of nature punching in on the time clock; while we're running out of younger workers, 85 percent of older workers want continued employment, at least part-time.

HIGH-FREQUENCY COOKING

If you find kitchen chores too difficult or time consuming, have you looked into microwaves? A microwave oven can give you a whole new outlook on cooking. The immediate advantages are speed, labor conservation, and energy efficiency—not to mention the fun of experimentation.

This new way of cooking creates virtually no heat in

the kitchen. Researchers at Cornell University have found that in general, nutritional value of foods cooked by microwaves is higher; fewer nutrients are lost or damaged during the short cooking time. Just think: a cornish hen in twelve minutes, a baked Idaho potato in five minutes, two slices of bacon in a minute and a half —*without* unpleasant cooking odors or greasy splatter.

The quality of food cooked by this method is higher than that of food heated by conventional cooking methods. Vitamin C, which is most susceptible to destruction by cooking, is as much as 50 percent better preserved in fruits and vegetables cooked ever so briefly by microwaves. Also, defrosting food at room temperature destroys more nutrients than are destroyed by using microwaves at the "defrost" setting.

You may be wondering if it is really safe. The U.S. Department of Health and Human Services and other federal agencies regulate and test microwave ovens; they are absolutely safe home appliances—safer than conventional ovens in some respects, because *only* the food gets hot—not the oven, not the dish. In *short,* it's the "new *wave*" for the busy or lazy, big and small households, kids, dieters, health food fanatics, you and me.

SUPERSTITION

It was George Jean Nathan, the drama critic, who is reputed to have said that superstition is "the belief that stage kisses give no satisfaction to actors or actresses." Though we may deny it, most of us have a set of built-in superstitions. Some we refuse to discard, even though we know better, because we're never *entirely* convinced that it's safe to do so.

Builders of high-rises still fear that the thirteenth floor may be the last to be occupied. Actors seem to have an abundance of superstitions, perhaps because we occupy a world of make-believe, where dragons are real and angels can speak. "Break a leg" is the parting shot before the curtain rises. In Germany they say "Neck and leg fracture." I'm not sure whether such tough-luck blessings are based on inherent jealousy among stars or on the belief that a bad break would be less dire than a bad review.

The final scene of the Broadway show *Steaming* might have engendered a new superstition for theater patrons: never sit in the front row without a raincoat. In one hilarious split second the onstage sunken pool in this bathhouse set is leaped into by three young actresses simultaneously, cannonball style!

Most superstitions actually derive from ancient folklore or religious rites. Breaking mirrors, for example, brings bad luck, probably because primitives felt their image shattered—for at least seven years. But how to figure out the superstitions attached to black felines? In theater circles these days nobody seems worried about them. After all, *Cats* is a number-one hit show.

I was introduced to backstage superstitions at the age of eight. Freshly up from Washington, D.C., in my first musical comedy, I shared the dressing room with the chorines. One evening there was a sudden commotion, much screeching and pushing: one chorus girl cussing the other; one crying while being pushed out into the hallway and turned around and around by her shoulders. What I learned was that whistling in a dressing room may bring instant dismissal to the cast member who happens to be standing nearest the door.

THE INITIAL GAME

Why is it that we despise street vendors on our avenues when we adore their quaintness in foreign lands? I find them amusing.

Walking down a side street in midtown Manhattan is akin to negotiating an obstacle course. Belts hang from wooden display racks; bags are spread out on an old blanket; briefcases are arranged like fallen dominoes. There are blouses on T-stands, sunglasses, folding umbrellas, and digital watches that tell the hour, date, and day—for only three dollars.

Suddenly there is a flutter, like pigeons startled by backfire, and all the young vendors scoop their wares into the display cloth, hoist them over their shoulders (or, occasionally, into a nearby van), and disappear. Frequent backward glances bespeak their knowledge of a policeman in the area whose sudden appearance has been announced, silently, by a lookout in their employ. This is democracy. In more ways than one.

Sold on the sidewalks are izod shirts, vanderbilt jeans, cardin watches, gucci wallets, givenchy handbags, and jordache belts, with lower-case initial letters, so to speak, because all are knockoffs and everyone knows it.

In our country snobs have a heck of a time being different. Housing developers put sunken Roman tubs into each bathroom. Car manufacturers put a check in the mail to designers who "autograph" the car. Lady Godiva finally got something from Bill Blass: his name is now on the box of pralines; a *BB,* poured in chocolate, is the pièce de résistance in the center of the fancy array of candies. Blass-phamous? Blass-famous?

Just a few years back status was collected from the army/navy store or the Salvation Army. Hairdos were don'ts, manicures cost $2.50. Today we spend thousands—in wardrobe finery alone—to send an eighteen-year-old, of either sex, off to college.

Irving Berlin's "Puttin' on the Ritz" is once again an international hit song. Does that tell us something?

Last Christmas a long-haired young man set up shop on his army blanket on the sidewalk in front of Cartier's great bronze doors on Fifth Avenue. "Gold chains—any one for a dollar." I was so impressed with his sense of merchandising that I bought one.

Part 4

We started out by planning
to change everything.
Now is not the time to cling
to what was, but to amend
what is.

"QUEEN VICTORIA" AT MAYO CLINIC

What is it like to find yourself growing old? That question was the basis of a dramatic presentation at the Mayo Clinic in May 1983. The focus: Queen Victoria, that extraordinary regent of England who ruled, in person and through her relatives, over most of Europe, politically and emotionally, for more than sixty years.

Together with my good friends Mildred Natwick and Fritz Weaver, I did a reading of passages from *Victoria Regina* for the staff of the Mayo Clinic. Queen Victoria was chosen as an example of an aged person who successfully surmounts several major crises and finds excitement rather than extinction in her later years. This presentation was arranged to help physicians and medical students gain empathy and understanding of common problems of the elderly.

From Cicero, we learned that "old age is honored only if it defends itself, preserves its rights, maintains its independence and rules its own realm." From Victoria, we learned that to retreat into the shadows, the black gown and mood, is an abdication not worthy of a queen, or any of us.

But even at the age of seventy, the proud "old girl" Victoria would not let a portrait artist paint her as she truly was; she could not understand that physiological aging can also be beautiful. Yet whenever she was confronted with aggressive behavior she asserted her identity—*regally*.

In the natural order of things, it is only for a time that the aloneness of widowhood obscures a natural need for companionship and human relationships—psychological, social, sexual. Dr. Wendell Swenson, professor of psychology at the Mayo Medical School, said, "The human arena is where the action is. We would do better to stay in the center of it, displaying our physical as well as our psychological battle scars rather than covering them with an embroidered shawl." In other words, he concluded, "We must remain on the 'cutting edge' of life's experiences, with our peers *and* with younger people."

AGING EGOS

What becomes fragile when we age is not our bodies so much as our *egos*. We don't *like* ourselves in the altered state. Why not? We *did* like growing up. We took pride in youthful body changes. We accepted the middle years—graying temples, laugh wrinkles, even a few extra pounds and inches. Now, must we dye our white hair and lift facial sag?

Self-denial is self-deceit. If we employ that kind of negative mentality, how can we expect to be received with open arms by the world out there? Wanting to lose track of time, as so many depressed elderly do, is a sure road to deterioration. Why look at old age as a personal insult? Older people who try to stem the tide of time only aid and abet those who despise aging. "I'm not getting any younger," we say when we want to retreat from reality. We use that old saw either to cop out or to grab all we can before we think it will be too late. Tell the truth; if you had one wish granted to you, would you really want to find yourself back at a long-past point in time?

The best way to adjust—no, ignore—most of the negative thoughts about aging is to say to yourself, with conviction, "I am still the *very same* person I have been all of my adult life." You *are,* you know. You haven't changed in the least. Yes, you may need glasses. And if you need a hearing aid, for heaven's sake, get one! Don't try to live with a script from the past in dealing with your present physical needs and possible impairments.

Remember, it's entirely normal to *maintain intellectual capacity for life*. You must believe in it, like Tinkerbell. It works!

DEVELOPMENT OF POTENTIAL

A friend of mine said the sad part about her late-in-life accomplishments is that her parents never got to see how successful she became. I'm sure this is happening to a lot of people today who don't really develop all their capabilities fully until they've experimented with life for a while.

That we must choose, at eighteen, what road to follow—and stay on that path until the end—has by now become an antiquated idea. We take it for granted that artists mature, that writers become more seasoned; that's true of all of us. But unless we try, unless we reject the thought that it's "too late," we'll never realize our potential. Part of the problem is adoration of youth.

I think we are notorious for placing reverential emphasis on the wrong decades of life (unlike the Chinese, who, I'm told, don't celebrate birthdays until their seventies!). It may well be that the invention of the camera is at the root of the youth cult. How utterly lovely are those young things jumping out at us from every magazine cover, TV screen, and billboard. Look in the mirror and you think you're from another planet. But the image reflected there has the benefit of *life* instead of the mastery of makeup.

Fortunately, though, attitudes are changing. The more that older people stay in the mainstream of life, the more accepting generations will be of each other. Whenever anyone wants to make a point about the accomplishments one can rack up late in life, a long list of *famous* people is mentioned. The fact is *ordinary* people do it every day, and they are the ones who'll make the greatest impact.

ADDICTION

On my birthday, a dear and very observant friend presented me with a candy bar he had had specially made for the occasion. It was the size of a golf bag, just about. A comic commentary on Helen's addiction!

Do you have any? Of course; we all do. Some, we conquer—some of the time. Some, we suffer with. And some of us are in real trouble because we can't cope with our personal addiction. When we read statistics on this subject, we learn that the cure rate is decimated by failure—numbers that reach 70 to 80 percent within a year. But one bit of encouraging news is provided by the folks who attempt to surmount their nemesis *on their own*—and succeed. However, they aren't counted in the graphs and percentages because they weren't part of a group or institution and were not under professional supervision.

Understanding the reasons for an addiction—with or without group support—is the basis for eventual control—self-control. People do manage to do it on their own, whether it's food, alcohol, gambling, spending, nicotine, sugar, or caffeine. Among all the friends I've watched over the years who've tried to quit smoking, I find that most of them finally succeeded. Having stopped and started more than once or twice only seemed to increase their determination. Just as in weight control, an occasional binge doesn't have to spell the end of the whole regimen. Whether you're working on your addiction by yourself, with a formal group, with medical help, or just with your friends and relations, take the same logical approach that Alcoholics Anonymous does: "one day at a time." And, as in A.A., a relapse doesn't mean failure.

You're a better person for having tried—and still better for starting again.

DRIVES AND MOTIVATIONS

It's been said that when you get older your drives and motivations decrease. Thank goodness! It's about time that the emotional, biological, and social machinery that sweeps you along for decades slows down so you can learn to enjoy it all.

The first thing you notice is that you keep telling yourself more often that you don't have to prove anything to anyone anymore. What a delicious release from the frenetic scramble for position and status. You've done it all; you've shown your worth, and now you can enjoy what you do—or do what you enjoy. Because now there is more time for everything, we can learn to become less compulsive, even about material possessions.

Let your acquisitive drive slow down to a crawl. You'll probably do your heirs a favor; they'll have less to quarrel over. You might even consider a program of what I call creeping divestiture. That's when you slowly and deliberately start giving things away. Start with the twelve lead-crystal plates you haven't used since your mother-in-law gave them to you.

If old Will Shakespeare had reached his retirement years, he might have said: This is the winter of our *real* contentment.

BETRAYAL

Radio soap operas and daytime TV sit-coms seem to leave nothing to the imagination. Anything goes. Everything is discussed. No thought is unspoken. Privacy plays no part. Along comes a startling new film written by Harold Pinter: *Betrayal,* the thinking person's soap.

Pinter unravels his plot in reverse! The film seems to be reeled into the can instead of out. You know the end before the beginning. What one doesn't notice, however, until long after we've left the theater, is that as viewer (or voyeur?), *we* are supplying the script. Ben Kingsley, the betrayed husband, is brilliant in his held-under, deliberate, measured portrayal. The lines spoken by all four of the cast are so meager, so innocuous, bland, and slow in coming that the audience is forced into supplying, mentally, all the missing lines, each according to his own way of thinking.

What made me think long and hard about Harold Pinter's view of marriage and friendship was the *unspoken* words. After you see the film *Betrayal,* you probably can make this observation yourself: we all do exactly that, every day, with everyone. We supply, in our minds, what we think the other *will* say, *should* say, *doesn't* say, or had better *not* say.

Is it possible that most of the emotional difficulties we have in our day-to-day interchange with others are precisely the words that are never spoken? We affect our relationships by supplying mental scripts of what we want or don't want to hear. If we could only learn not to fill in the blanks, imagine how much unnecessary trouble we could avoid. We could see and hear each other in reality.

AGE AND ART

I was impressed by an article in the New York *Times* aimed at all elderly would-be artists. The fact is that you can turn "would-be" into "I *am.*" A lot of older people have done it.

A second career is something to think about in the later years, when it's time to go on to something different, for example, painting, drawing, sculpting, or a craft. Let's meet a few people who made painting a second career at an advanced age:

Ivy Wood, formerly a cashier.
Sidney Manber, once a tailor.

George Whyte, civil engineer.
We shouldn't forget Rose Davis, formerly a
housewife.

All of them finally got around to what they wanted to
do most. Some of these painters are quite good; all of
them are getting an enormous amount of personal satisfaction and release of bottled-up emotions. You don't
have to be another Picasso to learn that painting is its
own reward.

One of the most important aspects is that you will be
looking at your world. Whether you're actually painting or just planning to, you will go around in your space
seeing things differently—the colors, the shapes, the
shadows, the seasons, the people. That's what makes it
rewarding. The final product is much less important.

Why not try it as an experiment yourself; carry your
camera around for a day as though you were on a trip
somewhere else. You will see things you've never noticed before. That's called *living!*

AMERICAN WORK ETHIC

When you watch young children at play, you will
notice that they're actually *working*. Piling up a tower
of blocks or digging in the sand "to reach all the way to
China" is hard work. Apparently children think work is
fun. Even the pressure to perform well or complete the
task is self-engendered. Take the little one who over-
turns his puzzle or sinks his boat in order to challenge
himself. To do it again, to solve the problem, becomes

the gratification. *Not* working is boredom beyond endurance, even for children.

What happens to change their minds? Probably the work they learn to resent so soon has been *imposed* on them and is not of their own choosing. To that, we then add the daily dinner table conversation—father's complaints about his job, mother's tales of drudgery and toil. A new attitude is formed in the young mind: work is awful.

We neglect to teach our children the pleasure of work and we rear them in an environment that doesn't encourage or admire hard work for its own sake. To get away with a minimum amount of work is the ideal. Leave it to machines, robots, services, gadgets, electronics, automatons. If we continue to fail our children, this negative approach to work will also stifle creativity and progress.

The satisfaction of working to the limit of one's capacity has to be reinstilled in our society. Those of us who are older and remember the time when everyone worked, children included, have a lot to contribute.

AUTOBIOGRAPHY

According to Professor B. J. Hateley, who teaches a writing course at the University of California, "The process of life-review is highly therapeutic—and the best way to get into it is to pick a theme." His course is entitled Psychological Development through Autobiography. His advice is to concentrate your outline for an opening chapter on a major turning point in your life or your family's history. To have a theme forces you to look at your life from a new vantage point. It helps to review the past in order to resolve old conflicts and arrive at a new understanding of yourself.

When we attempt to write our own stories—not necessarily for publication—we are, in effect, reaching for a very useful tool which helps us to come to terms with ourselves and, if we are older, with the prospect of death. Students who take this writing course range in age from twenty to eighty, and many of them are going through mid-life transitions.

Writing an autobiography has so many benefits: You are recording a private history for those who care about you and your family. Experts say it promotes self-esteem and personal integration. I think it clears away the cobwebs. Those memories we've pushed aside would become more accurate, less painful, if we were to record them as factually as possible. Writing stimulates a fresh new way of thinking and looking back on your life. It's interesting to note that Professor Hateley's students express no regrets over things they've done—only things they didn't do.

GRAND PERSON CONTEST

I've always been of the opinion that separating the generations is a gross injustice to all concerned. And now I have some written proof. There was a school essay contest, entitled Grand Person, in which schoolchildren were asked to write about an older person who has had an impact on their lives and who probably will influence them in the future. I have seen the winning essays.

There's nothing I can possibly add to the emotion and depth with which these youngsters express their kinship with *their* grand person—which, by the way, in all three first-prize essays, was the grandmother. Sixth-grader Rachel First—oh, I know she'll always be a winner—writes:

> My grandmother truly believes there's nothing in the world you can't do . . . that makes me feel that I'm going to do something *special.* She makes a difference in people's lives.

The junior high school first-prize essay was written by a young Vietnamese who's in an English as a Second Language program. If I thought I could learn to write like this teenager, Hao-Ton-Hoang, I'd go to school with him. Actually I'm sure no one teaches him how to express his feelings with such eloquence. About his grandmother, he wrote:

> When she was in the kitchen, busy with those two secret hands, I would taste these dishes with my eyes, their smell pulled my nose and tickled my teeth. Not only her food served us, but also her love —the love of tenderness, the love of truth. She said "Grandma is the stem of your heart." Her love has stored itself in my heart. Old people like my grandma are not wasted lives—but, maybe, they are lost secrets.

I'd like to suggest that if every school in the country were to have Grand Persons as a subject about which to write, retirement communities might go out of business and nursing homes would stand half-empty.

REPRIEVE

Whether or not we're consciously aware of it, we *all* do daily *programming* into our *personal* memory bank —the brain and nervous system. For elderly people, it's particularly important to do a little research in anticipation of failing health. Read Agnes de Mille's wonderful book *Reprieve;* you'll see what I mean. This world-renowned dancer suffered a paralyzing stroke a few years ago. Her intense struggle to rehabilitate her body sufficiently to overcome total helplessness is inspiring.

Although complete recovery is not always possible, devastating disability isn't necessarily inevitable. The messages to speak, walk, eat, and function already are programmed. To retrieve them when the system has been impaired takes willpower. You can improve your abilities and even your agility, *at any age.* For example, if you're right-handed, try brushing your teeth with the left hand. In a safe, familiar place see how many steps you can take backward. To improve your balance, stand on tiptoes, with your eyes closed. Read out loud to strengthen your voice; choose difficult material to challenge your understanding.

Agnes de Mille's doctor said that in times of serious crisis, it's often malaise which proves to be more dangerous to the patient than the physical malady itself.

TAKING MY TURN

A successful new musical revue off-Broadway is called *Taking My Turn*. Well, it's really not new. It was finished and ready to go *seven* years ago. The long delay was due to its subject, which was considered too unpopular at the time: aging!

The producer found that the public and even older people themselves had "bought" the notion that they are not very useful, interesting, or admirable. Today, attitudes are changing. That makes me feel really great —not only because good, original theater is being given a chance, but because my work (a daily radio program and other political and social action with which I'm involved) is contributing to this vital change in the climate. In the opening number of *Taking My Turn*, the cast approaches the footlights and asks, "Who's going to stop me if I start to sing?"

Robert Livingston is the adapter and director of this revue, which theater critic Clive Barnes said was "enormous fun." The night I was there, the whole audience agreed, young and old. The show is based on material contributed by the elderly—diaries, poems, one-liners, conversations. "It's a musical celebration of life," says one of the eight actors, a show about people who want to be part of life and "pick more daisies," to quote one of the lyrics.

Margaret Whiting, the distinguished vocalist, plays the role of a "survivor" type—a heroine of sorts—who says at one point, "Age doesn't make you boring; boring makes you boring." In a sad ballad about her dead son, she avoids all sentimentality. The result has a powerfully dramatic impact. She sums it up by saying, "The show couldn't get maudlin. We wouldn't let it."

WORDS

As children, we collected things—baseball cards, marbles, butterflies, greeting cards, matchbooks, stamps. Some of us collected words, written in a diary.

Acting, even in silent moments, conveys the written or spoken words of the playwright and director. In life, the words which guide—for some of us—are in our faith, personal or traditional. A few of the great many words which have made my life beautiful—or bearable —have been collected in a book called *A Gathering of Hope.* I preface each chapter with personal reasons and special feelings which I have for these selections— songs, poems, prayers, literary excerpts. Though the book has my name on the cover, I feel as though no name belongs there. There's none on the world's most universally read book of inspiration, is there!

Books don't have to be published in order to be of great value to an individual. Why not write a *private* book? It's a marvelous way to think and see more clearly—especially your relationships with others. You can begin by creating a personal clipping service. Collect words written by others that *reach* you—funny, touching, inspiring, clever, profound words. You might want to note why you chose each, how you felt at the time, how it expressed or clarified your own thinking.

When you look back over your scrapbook, you may

find a new and interesting "portrait" of yourself. Such "gatherings" were the inspiration for my last book.

WEATHER—WE LIKE IT

I've noticed that when nature deals us a real blow, it seems to change us from strangers into friends. When the temperature hits bottom, and our breath forms icicles in front of our eyes, people begin to see each other —and they smile as each reaches his quarter of a revolving door. When the thermometer hits the top, or rain is ankle deep, someone will hold the cab for you instead of slamming the door. When the wind whips up the mess in the street as if with an eggbeater, everyone feels a sudden surge of brotherhood. During a state-wide electric blackout, New Yorkers became so finely attuned to each other's needs, even the crime rate dropped sharply. Now, why do you suppose that's so?

I think, perhaps, it's a little like religion. Some force, bigger than we are, is in charge, for the moment, uniting us—*and we like it.* No person is in control. No group is to blame. As a New York *Times* editorial said, "Snow isn't caused by cruelty, or the Arctic air blown in by avarice."

Too much of what hurts us and divides us is our own doing. So we welcome problems that are in no way our responsibility. Buckminster Fuller spoke of this globe we're whirling around on as "Spaceship Earth" on which we are passengers. But we're more than that. We're the crew and the officers.

And perhaps there is a captain, after all.

TOUCHING

When we want to describe an emotion-packed scene or a great kindness, we use phrases like "it was so touching," "I was really very touched."

It's just recently come to the attention of the medical world—what the unsophisticated have always known—that touching is an absolutely vital part of physical and emotional well-being. Infants thrive. Pains subside. Healing takes place. Emotions are soothed.

The touch of another being isn't just a human necessity. It activates the biological mechanisms which help the body heal itself. It makes the mind like itself. Not just young lovers' heart rates change when they hold hands. It happens even to patients in a coma when they are stroked. In at least one hospital, volunteers hold, touch, stroke the very sick babies, with measurable results. As we know, women in labor whose husbands attend them are much eased by this contact.

One researcher who wanted to know how much touching goes on in some cultures came to the dismal conclusion that Americans touch about one fiftieth as much as some less uptight nations. We don't even shake hands when we meet or part. Men have a particularly strong "hands-off" attitude with each other. Yet new methods of photography prove that there's an "aura"— an "electronic field"—around each of us. The energy which flows from one person to another can be seen on film.

Dr. Dolores Krieger, a professor at New York University's School of Nursing, says that in the laying on of hands, energy is transmitted from her body to the patient. Perhaps our collective minds would ease and our bodies would benefit if we, as a nation, could get past the antiquated idea that touch must be either a sexual signal or an act of aggression.

RISK

Do you consider yourself daring? Well, perhaps now that you're getting older you've become more cautious. Maybe too cautious? If you've forgotten just how brave you used to be, look back at some of your adventures.

Marriage was probably the blindest step you ever took. I often wonder how we ever had the nerve to shed our parental security blankets and dive into a life we knew absolutely nothing about. What about childbirth? They say no woman would ever do it twice if she could *remember* what she went through! And child rearing? What did we really know about it? No one teaches *that* course in college! In our business or professions, we took risks that in retrospect appear overwhelming. But we did it.

And today? Have you become so cautious about your activities, your finances, your health—that you've come to a grinding halt? Many of us waste our days in fear of difficulties that *never* arise. The weather *wasn't* as bad as the forecast. The traffic *wasn't* a problem, after all. The distance *didn't* affect the plan. The crowd or noise *wasn't* too much. Your strength didn't fail you. You didn't forget. You didn't get lost. Your home was in *fine* shape when you got back. *And so were you.*

The benefits of having participated, having tried new

ventures—that is, really living—far outweigh the possibilities of failure or detriment to your well-being. Whatever you do, take the responsibility *yourself,* and don't let the opinion or disapproval of others influence your decision.

TO REST IS TO RUST

My approach to aging is at odds with that of the behavioral pyschologist B. F. Skinner. He believes in making concessions to growing old; give the old brain a rest! I, of course, refuse to slow down, lie down, or back down. Skinner says, "It's characteristic of old people *not* to think clearly, coherently, logically, or, in particular, creatively." To all of that, I say simply "bosh!"

And so, apparently, do these people:

A sixty-five-year-old who wrote, "I retired into more activity. I'm a go-go-go girl. I don't want to sit and vegetate."

A seventy-one-year-old who holds *two* jobs— full-time secretary in a private school and a temp for a doctor on Saturdays.

According to a New York *Times* report on a recent convention of the American Psychological Association, those who are in favor of slowing down feel "life is sweet when you stop to smell the roses. It's at its worst when you feel you have to fill every waking moment with activity so you won't have time to think." And I *do* agree with that, too. I love my roses, and I enjoy sitting and thinking. Yes, that is the good part of aging. Setting a slower pace, for some, is certainly wise and can be wonderful. What we will have to learn as biologists prepare to extend life span—perhaps to 150 years—is that our time on Earth has *more* than three periods— young, middle-aged, old. A long-living society will set a different pace, each according to moment and mind. Just as long as we don't disconnect!

FEAR OF FAILING

The most marvelous life training course I can think of is the *theater*. In this business, you learn *early in life* of the advantages of failure. Yes, you read me correctly— failing has its benefits: you become more elastic and less rigid and self-effacing if you learn to accept it as an essential aspect of living.

When you've put all you've got into an audition, and all you hear from beyond the proscenium is: "Next!" you'll either build your personal strengths or fall apart, like scenery after the final curtain. What you accomplish in life is in direct proportion to what you expect of yourself. If we greet each new challenge with a litany of our shortcomings and past failures, there isn't much we'll ever do to our *own* satisfaction.

The best time to take some daring steps is when you get older. You no longer have to account to a parent; you're not responsible for your children. Why shouldn't you change things if you want to? Why shouldn't you choose alternatives? The Reverend William Sloane Coffin, Jr., said, "Our greatest moral problem today is cowardice." Judaism says that despair is a great sin. Self-doubt and fear of failure are the leg irons that keep us chained to the wailing wall of *un*accomplishments.

FAMILY JEWELS

I admired my friend's antique cameo earrings. She told me that they were originally a wedding gift from her grandfather to her grandmother. When she gave birth to twin girls (one of whom was to become my friend's mother), the set was divided and made into pendants for the girls. On a special birthday, her aunt and her mother each gave her their pendants to reassemble as earrings.

As we reminisced, passing such stories back and forth between us, we realized that children rarely get to hear these anecdotes about family heirlooms they will someday own, pass along to their children, or even sell. Wouldn't it be a good idea to make a written or taped story of these remembrances? Just as it was fun to brag about your fabulous tag sale treasure ("the man had no idea of the value"), so is it important to know the history of that violin or the danger faced when the silver was brought through enemy lines.

True, not all stories about family valuables have drama. Nor was everything "bought for a song" or of great rarity. But, taken as a whole, what we surround ourselves with and carry with us for decades has sentimental value and tells the history of the family to some extent. Older family members should get together to reassemble the details. Often only the oldest was told that Grandpa's watch came from Ireland and not New

York. Or that this faded photograph is father's sister, not his mother.

If you were to embark on such a project of cataloging your heirlooms, you yourself would enjoy the memories, and your heirs would know more about their background and understand the value—financial or sentimental—of each item. And, most important, succeeding generations would know their ancestors *and* understand themselves better.

AGING ACTIVISTS

We are too job oriented in this country. I remember a woman at a party who literally cringed at having to admit to not having a paying career. She was "just a housewife"! That seemed to put her in a category similar to spinsterhood.

The older generation is bending the population curve in a new and unsettling manner. We are the burgeoning statistic—twenty-four million strong—and healthier than ever, thanks to science. What will we do? Find jobs? Every one of us? Take employment away from the young? Become wards of the state? Sit around and complain? Lay low until we are finally called to higher ground? I read in the paper that we are considered a threat to the nation's budget. Thirty percent of Medicare is spent on us, for instance—some of it needlessly, painfully, uselessly.

To prolong life unnecessarily by hugely expensive, highly technological medical devices for the terminally ill and very old is against nature. We are beginning to learn how to take care of our bodies and brains so that they will last longer and function better. The job older people have—a job they need not compete for—is to be Aging Activists.

Now, we must acquire a cheerful attitude, stop griping, and take charge of things. Claude Pepper can't do it alone. We *are* a formidable statistic. Just before "they" start whispering about how we are the cause of a staggering national indebtedness, let's pay our dues with actions—in politics, in volunteerism, in charitable works. It's not enough to grumble and grouse and write a few letters of complaint. More important is the support we can and must give *each other.*

The young are much too busy working on *prolonging life.* They can't stay home and care for us, can they?

ENJOY *NOW*

I'm having the best time, now! So late? you wonder. The advantage of being at this point in my life is that I look neither back nor forward—more than a few days at a time. I just enjoy *now.*

What that accomplishes is to eliminate the gnawing feeling one usually has about life rushing past. Because of yesterday, because of tomorrow, you can't take in all of today. Does this have to do with age? Not really. You can readjust your attitude at any time. Most of us let our ambitions, plans, or pressures to succeed stand in the way of "living." We are forever vaguely dissatisfied—with the moment, the surroundings, the people—*ourselves.* So busily do we pursue the "good life" that we don't recognize it when it's here. "I must take a long vacation," we say—while rushing around to make it possible.

Would your best-laid plans come to a grinding, irreversible halt if you took two hours for lunch, by yourself, to look at that polished sky today? Or wander through a museum? Or play with a child? Or make an extravagant long-distance call to someone who really matters to you? Of course not.

To feel really good about yourself, your life, you don't have to make the front page or make a million dollars. You don't need to be on a high—just being high on yourself will do very well.

What is your goal, your standard for success? If you're in your middle years, I bet you passed it several times and were so compulsively setting up higher hurdles, you never noticed or congratulated yourself.

All you really have, in the final analysis, is self-esteem. No one gives it to you. You can't buy it. It's not traded on the exchange. Most of us can explain, at great lengths, our dissatisfactions. But we fail to recognize and understand enjoyment.

Part 5

We relish news of our heroes, forgetting that we are extra-ordinary to somebody too.

GEORGE ABBOTT

To become a luminary with high visibility in the world of theater, it helps to have three things in your favor: talent, diversity, longevity. George Abbott is one of the wealthiest men in show business; he has all of these in huge abundance.

Born in the horse-and-buggy days of the Cleveland administration, he commutes to his beach home by private jet. How prolific his career has been takes twelve inches of column space, in tiny print, in *Who's Who in the Theater,* listing 120 shows on which he has worked, in seventy years, as author, producer, actor, director, and often as *more* than one of these.

Mr. Abbott *is* Mr. Broadway—six foot two, ninety-six years old. And active? What an understatement! George Abbott directed his first smash hit in 1926, which was quite appropriately called *Broadway.* By then, his career was already thirteen years in the making—writing, acting, stage managing. In 1936, he wrote *On Your Toes,* with Rodgers and Hart. In 1982, he rewrote it and directed it himself. It is still a smash hit. The most important thing for him is work. He says, "I think it's nice to wake up in the morning with a problem and be excited and try to do something." And when he's not working, he's playing golf or dancing. Other, privately held opinions about the quality of life: "I never think of dying. Smoking and drinking don't do you any good, and stress and hate are poisonous," he says.

This ninety-six-year-old legendary Broadway author-director was married last November for the third time, to fifty-two-year-old Joy Moana Valderama.

To be so full of life is an obvious prerequisite for putting great entertainment on the stage. The other is incurable optimism. What's your next project, George?

CHARLES AZNAVOUR

Best known among European *chanteurs* is Charles Aznavour—the most French among the French singers. There's something in that passionate voice that paints pictures of boulevards and Maxim's, champagne and children in sailor blouses. He epitomizes what we expect to hear when we go to a chic club—a "night box," as the French say. And yet Charles no longer frequents those spots for his own amusement. He and his wife, Ulla, prefer to spend evenings at home. When he concertizes, he writes his own songs and lyrics—some melancholy, some romantic, some satirical.

Innocence or foibles of young and old, lovers and freedom fighters, his observations of us all—these are his subjects. He has a healthy attitude about his own aging: he actually enjoys it. He lets his hair go gray and loves being a grandfather. One of his songs pokes fun at aging men in tight jeans, with their middles bulging over the belt line.

Aznavour is very much a product of his time. As so many who were soldiers in the second war or living in countries that were under attack, this sixty-year-old man thinks of himself as having been old at nineteen or twenty—in spite of his most famous song, "Yesterday,

When I Was Young." He says *now* he's young, much younger than he was then. His voice is strong and his outlook positive. His Armenian parents were so deeply involved in the horrors of the war years that he feels himself beyond involvement in the political side of life.

In a recent movie about Edith Piaf, Charles portrays himself as he was then—that "old man" of twenty-four or so—part of the Piaf clique in her heyday. So that is the advantage of keeping slim! You can play yourself in new movies about the old days.

Now, where did I put that calorie counter . . . ?

SID CAESAR

In the late 1940s and early 1950s, the highlight of the week was to be invited to a friend's house who already owned a TV. "Your Show of Shows"—*live* television. That's all it took to get you hooked for life. I wonder if that medium would have had such a phenomenally rapid growth without the folks who brought us *real* humor.

Sid Caesar was the emperor of that realm, and Imogene Coca his consort. Do you know who were the writers? This list of unknowns (then)—luminaries (now) —will surprise you: Mel Brooks, Neil Simon, Carl Reiner, Woody Allen. I need hardly tell you about them.

Until 1958, Sid Caesar was considered one of the funniest entertainers. He earned a million dollars a year then, but couldn't find the place where they sell happiness. As happens so often, the pressures of success overwhelmed him. Drugs and alcohol became the slow but sure avenue to disaster. Both his career and private life crumbled. His health deteriorated. Sid is interested in reestablishing his professional life, now that he has "found new and healthier addictions," such as exercise and writing. He says, "This disease is like an ulcer—it's nothing to be ashamed of. I'm still an alcoholic; you're never cured when you have an addictive personality. When I realized I wasn't the only one suffering, my entire perspective changed."

I hope Sid Caesar will come back to entertain us with *real humor*. I agree with him that throwing a pie isn't funny. *Not* throwing it is.

PERRY COMO

For those of us who first grew up with radio and then were enthralled by the early years of television, Perry Como ranks as one of the most pleasant memories. It is said that he is one of those great pop singers who is a complex mixture of voice, personality, sensitivity, and taste. Just about everyone feels he's with an old friend when Perry Como entertains. The apparent ease with which he presents his material belies the fact that hard work goes into it and that he wasn't "born" into the profession.

As one of thirteen children of an Italian immigrant family, he grew up in a small Pennsylvania coal mining town. By the age of ten, rather than go into the mines, he apprenticed himself to a barber. He opened his own shop at the age of fourteen. And it just seemed natural for him to croon while wielding the shears.

When the Freddy Carlone Band came through town in 1933, the barber, Perry Como, was discovered, offered a job, and went off traveling. That same year he also married his childhood sweetheart, Roselle. Just recently they celebrated their fiftieth wedding anniversary *and* his fortieth year with RCA Records—a "record" in itself. One hundred million Perry Como records have been sold worldwide. His drive to excellence is carefully camouflaged under the relaxed, easygoing style which has made him so lovable. A staggering list of his accomplishments fills volumes—big-band vocalist; teenagers' idol; major radio, TV, and film personality—a man with universal appeal.

Perry Como is one of those talents who is impervious to time. In the last two years he played four concerts in Manila, eight in Japan, did a Christmas special from Paris, released a new album called *So It Goes,* and played a number of golf tournaments, many for charity. There's no stopping this man!—to our great delight!

MARIE CURIE

Many women eventually face the problem of widowhood. We live *longer* than men. How we handle loneliness obviously is unique in each case.

Marie Curie spent many years alone, and they were her most productive ones. Marie, the Polish science student who married her French professor, became his partner in scientific research. Years and years of experimenting finally paid off in their great discovery: radium. The Curies worked together and triumphed together. They won the Nobel Prize for physics in 1903. When Pierre Curie died, his widow also lost her partner in science. But she was determined to continue with

the experiments they had planned. By herself, Marie
Curie isolated pure radium, which won her the Nobel
Prize for chemistry in 1911. Perhaps she is the only
woman ever to win the Nobel Prize two times.

And perhaps *you're* the only woman who has ever
won the senior singles tennis twice at your club! What's
the difference, so long as you enjoy what you're doing
and don't let the rocking chair get you. As you get
older, you learn to modify your activities and the demands you make on yourself. The trick is to *continue to
learn,* to *challenge yourself,* and to make some demands on your mind and body.

HENRY FONDA

After appearing in ninety-one movies and TV programs, Henry Fonda died, in 1982, at age seventy-
seven. Americans everywhere paid their respects to
this extraordinary man. It was a credit to the man and
the actor that there was little of the maudlin mourning
we commonly encounter when other celebrities die.
Fonda had become such an important part of the motion picture industry that most of us accept him as age-
less.

Sometimes it seems that a lot of weeping is done
when a person dies because of a life that didn't get *fully*
lived. Henry Fonda's heart gave out after he'd given
the best that was in him—after he'd performed his way
into a permanent niche in American moviemaking. His
films, like *Grapes of Wrath, Ox Bow Incident, Mr. Rob-
erts, Twelve Angry Men, Young Mr. Lincoln*—and his
last Academy Award triumph, *On Golden Pond*—are

part of American film history. We all identified with him, no matter the role he was playing.

His eyes were marvelous, reflecting his innermost feelings. They told the truth. How symbolic that Hank Fonda chose to will his eyes to the Manhattan Eye Institute. Henry was in and out of hospitals the last eighteen months of his life. He was partially deaf, had an arthritic hip, and some cancer going back to 1979; but still he played out his last role the way stage professionals wish to do. And even that last film, *On Golden Pond,* wasn't meant to be his farewell performance. Before he died, Fonda was searching for another script—an encore, if you will.

What a man. And what a lesson for us all.

DOROTHY SNELL FULDHEIM

Cleveland, Ohio, has an outstanding news analyst on its television station, WEWS. She is Dorothy Snell Fuldheim, who is past ninety. You may think this station is smart to realize that the "graying of America" is an undeniable fact and has, therefore, decided *now* to have this lady among its regular staffers. The fact is they've been smart for thirty-six years!

Fuldheim has become an institution on Cleveland television. She has even been named Ohio's Woman of the Decade. In 1912, Dorothy finished her training as a teacher. This career didn't appeal to her as much as professional acting, which eventually brought her to the lecture platform with Jane Addams, the pioneer social worker. Apparently she had a reputation for militancy, a feistiness which still comes through in her interview programs. Of course, before she was a star reporter, she made her mark in radio. She applies what she calls the honest approach to her reporting. She says she "never caters to the popular notion. When I analyze the news, I analyze it the way I see it. It may not always be logical; it may not always be correct; but this is the way I see it." She has interviewed every president since Franklin Roosevelt, and famous personalities from a young, hotheaded Jerry Rubin—to Einstein—to Zsa Zsa Gabor, and, incidentally, me. What has made this such a long association with just one TV station? "They took a gamble with me," she says. Though there have been other offers, loyalty keeps her with her first boss. Dorothy arrives at WEWS at 9:30 every morning and stays till 6:30 P.M. And yet she finds time for lectures and appearances on other talk shows.

"Some of us have the kind of bodies that last longer," she says. And minds, I think!

BUCKMINSTER FULLER

"There's nothing in a caterpillar that tells you it's going to be a butterfly. Who knows what *man* can become?" The man who said that became a scientist, inventor, historian, philosopher, engineer, poet, mathematician—but also cartographer, cosmogonist, designer, choreographer—all in one lifetime of eighty-seven years.

Most of us know of him as inventor of the geodesic dome—R. Buckminster Fuller. He said, "Man can create anything he needs. Man *can* create a miracle." Fuller created the legend he was. Although he was never formally educated in architecture, his designs were revolutionary, world-renowned. The triangle, basis of the geodesic dome, constitutes one of the most stable structures in the world.

Bucky Fuller believed single-mindedness obscures integrity. He represented that element in human endeavor which is almost always missing: *his* ideas took in the *whole* of man's environment, experience, history, and potential.

He held more than two thousand patents; he wrote twenty-five books, including three acclaimed volumes of free verse and one called *Operating Manual for Spaceship Earth,* because he believed each of us must become familiar with its mechanics to keep it operating. To make his point, he reminded us that when he was a boy in the 1890s, 95 percent of the people on the planet were illiterate. Today, 65 percent still are illiterate. At a low point of his personal life, when he considered suicide, he pulled himself back into reality by deciding to discover the principles operative in the universe and turn them over to his fellow men.

ARTHUR GODFREY

CBS Chairman William Paley once said of Arthur Godfrey that he was "the average guy's wistful projection of what he would like to be!" The gravelly voiced radio personality became Mr. Television to most of us when we first acquired that unwieldy one-eyed box, which has dominated our living rooms and our lives ever since.

Arthur was amusing, he was friendly, he looked right

in your eyes from under those red eyebrows. He sang little ditties and strummed the ukelele. Most of all, he sold us things that, according to him, we could live without, but shouldn't—and which made him, in turn, exceedingly rich. He made us feel good and, sometimes, embarrassed us, right there, in front of millions, on live television. When he was fifty-five, his lung cancer and surgery caused a national vigil. His so-called retirement didn't last. He said he gave up only cigarettes and tap dancing.

When Arthur Godfrey died in March, 1982, I heard a rebroadcast of his narration of President Roosevelt's funeral. His choked voice still had the same emotional effect on me. In the heyday of his career—from 1945 to 1959—Arthur almost dominated radio and television, with an estimated audience of 82 million. The secret of his success was his personal intimacy—his style of talking to the listener as though the other 82 million weren't in the room. Although Arthur was not a simple man, or even uncommonly good or kind, he made us believe in him and in an honest, open, old-fashioned life, which neither he nor we were part of anymore.

LOU GOSSETT, JR.

Sometimes we see a great performance on stage or screen by a mature actor and we ask, where has he been all this time?, when actually we have seen him many times before.

Louis Gossett, Jr., is one of those fine actors who is a victim of his own versatility; he disappears so completely into whatever role he plays that we don't con-

nect him to his long list of successes. As the tough
Marine drill sergeant in *An Officer and a Gentleman,*
he can hardly be forgotten. It won him an Academy
Award for Best Performance by an Actor in a Support-
ing Role. He is the first black actor ever to win in that
category.

Lou is no newcomer. He's been in the profession for
thirty years and, as a teenager, was named Broadway's
Best Newcomer of the Year. We have all seen him many
times and marveled at his talent: dozens of leading
roles in plays and TV movies, including an Emmy-win-
ning performance in *Roots.*

Lou Gossett's personal story would make a good
drama. Acting was an accidental choice for him. He had
planned on becoming a brain surgeon. His father
worked his way up from porter to chief of the mailroom
at the Brooklyn Gas Company. His great-grandmother
lived with them until the age of 117. Lou's mother
heeded his request to quit domestic work and return to
school to earn a degree. At the time of her death, she
was being put up for assemblywoman. Lou's formal
education went as far as premedical studies at New
York University, for which he had been granted a schol-
arship. He played basketball as a star among future all-
stars. But acting was already in his blood since high
school, and he picked up some Broadway credits while
still at college. In 1983, we saw him in a key role in *Jaws
III* and also enjoyed his portrayal of Sadat in the four-
hour miniseries about the slain Egyptian president.

Performer, director, teacher, humanitarian—a powerful man who can no longer disappear completely into
his role. We must recognize him!

KATHARINE HEPBURN

The theater has always been a powerful influence on the attitudes of the public. Morals and mores can be improved—or they can be destroyed—by a rash of theater pieces with a particular slant. Most plays, sooner or later, turn into movies for all the world to see.

Broadway has been doing a string of plays in recent years which deal with the elderly, for example, *Morning's at Seven, The Gin Game, The Sunshine Boys.* One of the world's best-loved actresses starred in *The West Side Waltz*—the indomitable Yankee, Katharine Hepburn. Her own strength and joy for living flow from the stage to the audience, no matter what the lines or plot ask of her.

Aside from the great admiration I have for Katharine Hepburn, I love the fact that she played the part of a strong, willful woman who will not let life defeat her and resents those who do. Claudette Colbert's recent appearance in *A Talent for Murder* unfortunately placed the aging star in a wheelchair throughout the play. I prefer to see my contemporaries portrayed in more active roles. When a character in Katharine Hepburn's play warns her not to go out walking on a cold day, she announces, *"I'll run"*—as only Kate can say it!

Hurrah for Hepburn. She's giving the image of old folks a face-lift. I hope she will do the film, too. We *need* that kind of PR on *our side* of the mountain!

BOB HOPE

Only people who are *young* should think about their retirement. Once you get to be of "that certain age," try to avoid the thought, if at all possible.

Bob Hope, who is now past eighty, is one of those in our business who knows he needs the audience, the applause, the excitement, and yes, even the hassles of being in show business. Every time *I* take on a new assignment or another appearance, I kick myself a little right after the contract signing. Can't I learn to say no? No.

Maybe it's saying yes that leads to the positive approach, and kicking ourselves a little keeps the motor turning over. Many people who enjoy their work really miss it when they give it up. Boredom and frustration take over, and often not enough other interests existed with which to begin a new way of life.

What we can learn from Bob Hope's activities is that motivation has to come from within. After all, this wonderful performer could hardly be working for the money; he's one of the richest entertainers in the world. This is how he puts it: "I've always wanted to continue to get a laugh. It makes *me* feel good when I make a lot of folks in the audience feel good." Bob's been more active than ever. He's playing colleges, universities, performing at benefits and state affairs, theaters, clubs, and hotels. He raises funds and entertains veterans, produces and stars in full-hour TV specials, hosts the Hope Golf Classics, and makes star appearances on all the top TV shows around the country.

Bob's always between planes and dressing rooms, but he'll never fall between the boards. Because for Bob Hope, the stage is the world and laughter is the oxygen he breathes.

ALBERTA HUNTER

One of the most engaging performers is still holding forth in Greenwich Village—Alberta Hunter, the blues singer incarnate! Literally! Alberta Hunter is eighty-nine years old and is no stranger to the stage. She was a star and a recording artist in the Roaring Twenties, a black American who toured the world, spreading her particular inspiration, from the sensual to the serene. She retired from the stage in her fifties and became a much loved and loving practical nurse.

After having spent twenty-three years nursing at a New York hospital, and with no thought of giving it up in spite of her eighty-two years, Alberta Hunter was forced to retire. Too bad for the patients. Great for the rest of us—because now Alberta Hunter is singing again and we can all hear her, in person or on recordings. With her wonderfully strong contralto, she'll belt out "The Dark Town Strutters Ball," or become mellow with "Georgia on My Mind." She'll snap her fingers when she sings "Gimme That Old-Time Religion"; and between numbers she lectures her adoring audience with motherly admonitions: "call your parents"—"save some of your pay"—"weigh your words before speaking"—and, "children who cut school are cutting their own throats." She really *feels* young people's need for guidance, she says.

And perhaps it's true that what an audience needs today—amid all this crass realism—is some of those "old time lyrics" that make you glad, or sad, but not so awfully mad.

DANNY KAYE

If you don't believe it's possible to become the world's *most* famous entertainer in thirty-eight seconds, you don't know how Danny Kaye got his start. In Kurt Weill's Broadway show *Lady in the Dark,* Moss Hart inserted some lyrics which required rattling off the names of fifty Russian composers in thirty-eight seconds. I'm not sure there *are* fifty Russian composers, but Danny did it!

Remarkable things are what he does—like visiting sixty-five United States and Canadian cities in five days to celebrate the twenty-fifth anniversary of UNICEF. For this feat of logistics, he piloted his own jet and earned an entry in the Guinness Book of Records. He has raised over $6 million for musicians' pension funds by conducting orchestras, without ever accepting a fee for his services. The list of awards with which Danny Kaye has been honored could fill a small telephone book, including medals from heads of state and France's top culinary award, which only twenty-six chefs have ever received. He is also an expert chef of the food of every region in China; he once prepared such a dinner for me.

Among all his gilt-edged awards, though, one is missing: a high school diploma. Danny Kaye was a dropout. Perhaps that's how he's found time to do so many things so well. During the three years prior to his decision to move into television on a regular basis, Kaye was typically busy and typically ubiquitous: he made his first Las Vegas nightclub appearance; did a TV special; starred in a picture; toured the Orient on behalf of UNICEF; made a USO holiday tour of Japan and Korea; performed as a guest conductor with the orchestras of Boston, Detroit, Los Angeles, and Washington; visited Russia at the behest of the State Department; headlined theater bills in Honolulu, Denver, Washington, and other major cities; and took in a lot of ballgames.

Danny pilots his plane to take his mind off his work and has been known to take the controls of a 747 or a DC 10. Healthy, vigorous, restless, inspired: Danny Kaye is the world's ambassador of happiness.

ALAN JAY LERNER

Weeping our way through a box of tissues at movies is becoming extinct. Playwrights don't reach us emotionally the way they used to.

Alan Jay Lerner, the sixty-five-year-old librettist, says that "in a good musical, you reach a moment when you're touched, when a song reveals one person's deepest emotion." He's talking about what he calls "book musicals"—those which we all loved so much because they told a story—had a beginning, a middle, an end. That outdated construction, a *plot!* Lerner says that the star system has fallen by the wayside. The names of producers, directors, designers, choreographers are the ones up in lights now. His own legacy to theatergoers around the world, of course, includes *Brigadoon, My Fair Lady, Gigi,* and *Dance a Little Closer.*

Librettists, according to Alan Jay Lerner, are an endangered species. Perhaps that explains why revivals in the theater are very often those fine old storytelling musicals, like *Showboat, Fiddler on the Roof,* or *Man of La Mancha.* The audience is young—young enough not to have seen it before. And they love it!

I'm surprised that this need for involvement of the audience with the characters isn't obvious to every playwright. Why else are interview shows on TV and radio phone-in shows so popular? People want to have a peek at *other* people's lives. Alan Lerner said that the best musical he's seen in years was Yves Montand in his one-man show. "It was," he said, "the most totally satisfying evening of beauty. I wept just for the joy of seeing it. Montand made you know what people felt, and how their lives ran. That's what musical theater can be, and what it should be." Encore, Alan!

LOUIS ROTHSCHILD MEHLINGER

Louis Rothschild Mehlinger retired from an active law practice—just before his hundred and first birthday, I think. He said then he's asking the court to put him on the inactive list. While they were at it, I hope they also put his name on the top of the most active list. You'll see what I mean when I tell you a little about Louis, son of a German immigrant father and freed-slave mother, born in Louisiana in 1882!

This highly erudite gentleman says he has only one serious regret in his life—that he and his wife had no children to whom to transmit their achievements and learning. How young people could benefit from comprehending this little anecdote: As a youngster in boarding school, Louis was assigned to help care for a visitor from Toogaloo—Booker T. Washington. "I will never forget," Mehlinger said, "I got to shine the dear gentleman's shoes."

If only more people—especially the young—could consider it a lofty ideal to have had the chance to polish the shoes of a fine human being! Mehlinger didn't think of it as demeaning. He made his way up the ladder of education and career opportunities little by little—against great odds—by sheer willpower. It wasn't until his fortieth year that he graduated, magna cum laude, from Howard University's law school. But in those years having reached this degree of competence was no dooropener for even the most qualified black attorney. Louis said, "Many of us worked at very ordinary jobs, as clerks and messengers in the day, and went to our law offices in the afternoon, to work late into the night." By 1922, he was promoted to assistant attorney—a position he held for thirty years, followed by thirty more years of private practice.

That's a *long* way to go from being a stenographer in the days of Theodore Roosevelt. But Louis Mehlinger had a century to do it!

WORTHINGTON C. MINER

What makes television a very young art form is the fact that its golden age was only as recent as the 1950s. That was a time for experimentation—some wonderful shows evolved, which make much of today's TV fare seem puny by comparison.

I identify one man in particular with those bright years—Worthington Miner. What a full, active, inventive life he led in his eighty-two years! His TV credits virtually make up early TV history. He created "Studio One" and the TV version of "The Goldbergs." Remember "Toast of the Town," with Ed Sullivan? "The Play of the Week" and the "Kaiser Aluminum Hour"—real drama, every week. For "Studio One," Worthington Miner developed his own technique, combining recordings, for unspoken thoughts, with live and filmed sequences. Those were the days of live entertainment —no retakes, no editing.

Tony, as he was known to his friends since his school days, began his theatrical career as a spear carrier in *Cyrano de Bergerac* at the opera. In the 1930s, he directed many Broadway plays, among them *Jane Eyre,* which starred Katharine Hepburn; *On Your Toes,* with Ray Bolger; Alfred Lunt and Lynn Fontanne in Robert Sherwood's *Reunion in Vienna.* If you were a kid during TV's infancy, you remember "Mr. I. Magination," "Medic," and "Frontier," with Richard Boone. They were all Tony Miner shows.

About show business inequities, he said, "When we speak of the theater, we speak of one city—New York. Yet, even within the confines of that one city, the theater isn't democratic. It's a Park Avenue nightclub, a luxury for a select few. It's for the rich in the richest city. And, I believe this situation is deplored by every author, actor, and manager in the business."

Times haven't changed very much, have they?

ROBERT MITCHUM

Somehow I can't quite picture Robert Mitchum sitting on a flowered chintz-covered sofa in his living room—chinos and leather jacket—the inevitable cigarette clamped between his fingers. What is less incongruous is his voice—gruff, with modification—and his general demeanor: just as you've always seen him.

At sixty-seven, he's not much changed from my earliest recollections of him in films like *The Story of G.I. Joe, Not As a Stranger,* and *The Sundowners.* In *That Championship Season,* he is the team's beloved coach. In fact, Mitchum has lived the life he often portrays—simple, rough, unassuming, honest, kind. He has been a prizefighter, a scriptwriter, a shop worker, and a rancher of Thoroughbreds. The smoker's cough is real, the raised eyebrows permanent. The shape of the nose was altered in the ring, long ago. He continues to work in films and made-for-TV movies, but, compared to other actors, he's very relaxed—laid back—and totally noncompetitive.

The up-scale life of Bel Air (where Robert Mitchum used to own a home) and the fast folks of cinemaland don't suit him. He prefers the hills of Montecito and lives in a modest ranch house with his wife, Dorothy. They've been married since 1940 and have produced two actors and one scriptwriter: Jim, Chris, and Trina. One of Mitchum's co-stars was Marilyn Monroe, in *The River of No Return.* They had known each other in their pre-Hollywood lives when he and Marilyn's first husband were partners on the assembly line at Lockheed. He says, "She was a Valley housewife then, married to a red brick of an Irishman, who later became a cop. It was not a match made in heaven."

The word "type-casting" takes on a new meaning when you think of it in connection with him. Did he create Robert Mitchum—or did the studio?

ALVA REIMER MYRDAL

It's too bad that Alva Reimer Myrdal is almost as old as I am. I would have enjoyed portraying her life story in a movie. But this remarkable Swedish woman of eighty doesn't seem to be ready to close the book on her accomplishments. If I were to list her credentials, it would take pages.

Alva began as a teacher and director of teachers' colleges in Sweden. In 1949, she was head of the United Nations Department of Social Welfare and, later, director of its Educational, Scientific, and Cultural Organization. She even was Sweden's ambassador to India and minister to Burma and Ceylon.

Since 1961, when she was fifty-nine years old, disarmament has been her main preoccupation. At that time, her government asked her to take the post of special assistant on disarmament to the Swedish foreign minister. She felt strongly about it, but unprepared for the task. So she steeped herself in the subject for two weeks. After holding additional posts as a member of Parliament, delegate in Geneva, and cabinet minister, she finally resigned in 1973 so she could continue to write and lecture in her quest to ease the problems of the world.

In 1982, Alva Myrdal received the Nobel Peace
Prize. She once said, "If you have a chance to reform
things, don't you think you should?" She and her late
husband, Gunnar Myrdal, are the only couple who have
ever won two Nobel Prizes, each in a different field.
Gunnar's prize, in 1974, was in economics. They did
collaborate on projects, notably the book *Crisis in the
Population Question.* What kept their marriage going,
in spite of long career separations, was the deep interest in each other's work. She said, "We never found
anybody else so interesting to talk to."

Her influence on her country is responsible in part
for its welfare state, population control, women's rights,
and child care. Alva's motto? "I have never allowed
myself to give up."

MINNIE PEARL

Sarah Ophelia Colley Cannon is well-known to you
and me—as Minnie Pearl. This remarkable entertainer
is still working in radio, television, and music halls.
She's been Minnie Pearl for forty-four of her seventy-
two years. I once received a letter from Minnie in her
own strong handwriting:

Dear Helen:

*I have been known as Minnie Pearl for 42 long
and happy years. "She" has kept me young in
spirit! I thank God every day for her, bringing
laughter to audiences, as a stand-up comic. All
these years have not been easy, but the rewards are
tremendous.*

My pace has slowed very little, as I have gotten older. I'm still a regular on the TV show "Hee Haw" and on "The Grand Ole Opry," make commercials, and appear at concerts.

In between all these activities, I try to keep a home going for a delightful husband I've been lucky enough to have for 35 years. He's a pilot and has flown us many thousands of miles in our own plane. He's my personal and business manager, and I couldn't do it without his encouragement and support.

The years have flown by so fast that, fortunately, I've never been aware of growing old. By keeping busy, with the God-given bonus of having good health, I've really never given age a thought. I love my memories, which I recently compiled in an autobiography. My abiding faith in God allows me to look forward to many happy, active years.

Love,
Minnie Pearl

Well, if Minnie Pearl has her "druthers"—Lord willin'—she'll be doing for the rest of this century what she's been doing: making people happy.

CLAUDE PEPPER

You have an energetic voice in Washington, D.C., aptly named Pepper—Claude Pepper, chairman of the House Select Committee on Aging and a well-seasoned politician. I recently had the pleasure of attending a dinner party with him. At age eighty-two, he can deliver a primer on any subject: good manners, good law, good intentions—and his remarks never come off as a rebuke.

Claude Pepper is regarded as a spokesman for America's "maturians" (a word I prefer to "elderly"). But Congressman Pepper carries and expresses himself as a forty-year-old might. He's a proud man and he takes special pride in prodding the rest of us, debunking the myths about growing old.

Pepper sponsored a bill which eliminated mandatory retirement age for most federal employees, and raised it from sixty-five to seventy for workers in private industry, admonishing all of us that "the only mandatory requirement is when you can't do the work anymore." Bravo, Congressman!

Social Security was penalizing widowed beneficiaries who preferred remarriage to dual housekeeping arrangements, until Claude Pepper helped put a stop to that. This is his slogan: "Ageism is as odious as racism or sexism." He's determined to prevent Social Security cuts.

Thirty-six million people depend on his tireless efforts on their behalf. Remembering his own hard life as the oldest child of Alabama farmers helps him in his ceaseless efforts to alleviate the misery of the poor. Claude Pepper's aim is to better the lives of ordinary people. He continues to run for office and has now been made chairman of the House Rules Committee—one of Capitol Hill's most influential jobs.

As an active maturian, I myself intend to keep working until . . . well, perhaps the turn of the century, which I plan to celebrate on my feet! Claude Pepper is so right. If you have the capability and the *will*, don't quit! Last year I starred in a motion picture for television. My radio series, "The Best Years," airs every weekday in many cities, year-round, and my speaking engagements dot the calendar from one season to the next.

But you know, I sometimes think that Claude Pepper and I are speaking to the wrong audience. The lessons we've learned are better directed to people in their thirties and forties. Heaven knows, I meet so many young people who seem to have "retired" from this planet and are merely spectators, plugged into that TV box that thinks and acts for them.

As *Time* magazine pointed out, "While Claude Pepper's body has required a few repairs, his mind remains sharp, his memory so keen that he can be introduced to seven people at lunch, and thereafter address them unerringly by name." As one senator put it, "Pepper has reversed the aging process—and has more political clout now than ever!"

JASON ROBARDS

How often we admit, regretfully, that we didn't have enough time for our children! In time, as we get older, perhaps a little wiser, and certainly less compulsive, we all could probably be better parents.

That's how Jason Robards views *his* relationship with his first four children, who are now grown up. His two younger ones—still in their preteens—have a more mellowed man for a father. Now past sixty, Jason is no longer the hard-driving, career-building actor.

Children have a universal kinship in one respect—they're usually raised by two young people who have a lot of other important things to cope with—money, ca-

reers, establishing roots, creating a workable relationship between themselves, and often concern for their
own parents. There will never be a satisfactory solution
to that, although having children later in life is becoming more popular.

Jason Robards deserves a little peace in the stormy
life he's led. Hollywood was his hometown (his father
was also an actor). As a young man in the U.S. Navy
Reserves, he endured the attack on Pearl Harbor and
survived the sinking of his ship. He chose acting as a
career for himself, even though he'd seen what agony it
had caused his father.

It wasn't until 1956, in Eugene O'Neill's *The Iceman
Cometh*, that Jason Robards began to surface from the
eleven-year-long "don't call us, we'll call you" talent
pool. Long intervals between the successes, several
marriages, and too much liquor made for self-doubt. In
1972, he had a gruesome, near-fatal car crash. Just as
the surgeons reconstructed his body, so he rebuilt his
emotional life. Eventually he taught himself total sobri-
ety.

Today, Jason Robards would rather do stagework. (He
doesn't consider films to be "acting.") Just the same, I
still look forward to his next movie.

ARTHUR RUBINSTEIN

The man who might best exemplify the best of the
best years was Arthur Rubinstein. This brilliant piano
virtuoso, perhaps one of the three or four greatest of
the century, died at ninety-five. He performed profes-

sionally until he was ninety. What kind of spirit—inner strength—did this keyboard genius possess?

Any artist who schedules nine concerts in seven weeks at Carnegie Hall is taking on quite an assignment; he did this when he was eighty-one! He was so much more than an artist. He had an intense joie de vivre, enjoying his *life* because he loved his *work!* And he had fun. When asked for his recipe for zestful living, he said, "Eat a lobster, eat a pound of caviar—live! What good are vitamins? If you're in love with a beautiful blonde with an empty face and no brains at all, don't be afraid. Marry her! Live!"

Rubinstein's performances onstage were always electrifying. He bounced up and down, pounding the keyboard, then softening the texture of his playing for contrast. He was all of five feet eight inches, but he appeared as a giant among his colleagues, most of whom passed away decades ago. Music critic Harold Schonberg reminisces: "Rubinstein gloried in playing the piano. He was an extrovert, a 'ham,' if you will. But, fortunately, he had pure musical instincts and allied to his undoubted theatricality was a mind that saw the architecture of a piece of music, the correct shape of a phrase, the nuances that lie beneath the printed note."

A porter carrying a pail and mop once watched Rubinstein seated at the piano, practicing for a concert, and asked, "Do you do this professionally?"

CHARLES SCHULZ

Cartoons are like poetry. Perhaps more so. A few strokes with a pencil or india ink tell a story, echo a sentiment, awaken a memory, affect the reader. No words at all are needed. The emotional response is personal: "Yes, that's me!" We look at a cartoon or comic strip and laugh because it strikes a familiar chord, or because we didn't know other people felt the same way, too. It's a form of consciousness raising; group therapy.

The man who excels at this popular art form is, of course, Charles Schulz—the Charlie Brown in our lives. Funny, poignant, touching. Why *does* the Peanuts Gang make us feel so good? Because their creator feels that good when he puts his ideas on paper. There's nothing forced about this humor, no deprecating swipes, no self-inflicted pain.

Charles Schulz is known as "Sparky" to his friends and associates. His staff, who manage a very large organization, do not engage in the actual drawing of the cartoon strips. Schulz does that all himself and all ideas spring from him. At fifty-nine, he recovered from quadruple bypass heart surgery and was back exercising and working full-time at Creative Associates, his company in Santa Rosa, California. He lives the kind of life his character Linus wishes for himself: very rich, very humble, very normal, very famous.

Being a good person is what comes through in the work Schulz puts forth, *every day.* I do believe it has a great influence on his public. What pleases Schulz most about his phenomenal success is that it makes him one of the most famous people ever to graduate from his high school. That's one way to look at success!

ANDRÉS SEGOVIA

Guitar music is folk music in many parts of the world —and considered easy to play—except in the hands of Andrés Segovia. Only then is it given its full potential— the freedom to soar.

Segovia has been teaching himself to play since he was eight. There were no classic guitar teachers in his hometown in Spain; yet no other instrument was to his liking. He says the guitar never forgets its Spanish personality, or its femininity, comparing it to the soft curves of a woman. Now that Segovia is past ninety, you might imagine he needs to practice less arduously. On the contrary. He feels he must practice more—at least five hours a day—because while a younger artist might be forgiven a slip due to inexperience, not so the master! He no longer teaches, but eight or ten of his former pupils have become great artists in their own right. The rest have become guitar teachers in conservatories around the world.

Segovia has been on the road since he was fourteen and still travels extensively, giving many concerts. "Playing," he says, "helps my health, my mind, my heart . . . many things." Though he has never commissioned a work to be written for him, his popularization of classic guitar music has inspired composers to add more than three hundred pieces to the guitar repertoire. To have heard their work played, by what Spaniards call "the golden hands" of Segovia, makes them devoted composers for guitar.

The four tasks Segovia set for himself long ago still keep him occupied:

> to redeem the guitar from the tavern
> to create a repertoire of serious music by
>   symphonic composers, and not guitarists
> to travel and show the beauty of the guitar
> and, finally, to establish a curriculum for guitar
>   at the same dignified level as other
>   instruments.

He still works at these tasks each day. "I don't want to rest," he says. "I'll have an eternity to rest, later."

RUTH WARRICK

We have communication with the speed of light, transportation at supersonic pace, and yet we are more isolated, as individuals, than ever before. Being part of an "extended" family and having a large circle of friends is a rarity today. People are too mobile and too involved with their own lives to acquire the kind of tight relationships of former times—grandparents, cousins, aunts, uncles, and friends—when everyone lived close by, always available. What takes the place now of this important social structure, which has always nurtured and supported the human family? Soaps.

More people know and *care* about what happens to Phoebe Tyler than could ever have been predicted. Each week perhaps as many as fifty million people wait anxiously to find out how things are with Phoebe. *(And with themselves, perhaps?)* Do soap operas hold up a mirror for us to see how *we* are leading our lives? And do scriptwriters push just a little further each month to see if the public can bear it?

Ruth Warrick, the Phoebe of "All My Children," has a long and successful career in radio, TV, and film. She played *Citizen Kane*'s wife, but her public image did not emerge then (as one might have expected), because the powerful newspaper chain whose chief this motion picture portrayed suppressed all press mention of the film and its actors. Many good pictures and long-running radio serials have shaped Warrick's acting career since then. But she is also a bestselling author; recording artist; teacher and consultant on public works and charitable programs, lending her name, her time, and her efforts to such worthwhile organizations as Operation Bootstrap in Watts County, Los Angeles. She was a consultant to three presidents on school dropouts and job training. Currently she devotes energy to the education of autistic and disturbed children and the establishment of arts programs in schools and other humanitarian endeavors.

Quite obviously, Phoebe Tyler and Ruth Warrick are two *very different people.*

When "soaps" were still called "soap operas" and were fifteen-minute programs on radio, listeners were equally addicted but perhaps more attuned to the characters' fictitiousness. Each chapter was short, much less personal, and the cast of characters had to be created by the mental images of each listener. Emotions, problems, pleasures, fears—it had all that, but by intonation of voice and word only, not through the power of the camera.

Seeing is believing, I'm afraid. And all too many folks take the goings-on of soaps all too seriously. Is it perhaps too much to bring such powerful theater into every

home, every day, for hours on end? Does it permit
people to lead their own lives realistically?

LEONARD WIBBERLEY

I finally got to see a photograph of Leonard Wibberley. He looked exactly like I hoped he would—a
crinkly bearded woodsman or tall Rumplestiltskin with
an impish grin, as though he knew the magic secret that
unlocks the castle gate. He was the author of a hundred
books, including the hilarious satire *The Mouse That
Roared*. It's a story about the unfortunate occurrence of
winning a war—inadvertently—against the United
States.

Leonard Wibberley! What's in a name? A lot, in his
case! His given name made him "the lion hearted." His
surname was certainly whimsical, don't you think? A
great combination for a man whom one critic called a
"roaring philosopher" and who, according to another,
had a "snorting disdain for the status quo."

Leonard Wibberley was apparently also something of
a mystic. After his first heart attack and multiple bypass
surgery, he made the following observation: "They
brought my body back, but a different person inhabited
it. This stranger hated writing, hated music, couldn't
stand to be with his family and friends."

Well, that remark was indicative of this prolific writ-
er's insight into human nature—if not a look into the
beyond. Everyone who goes through a traumatic event,
physically or psychically, emerges changed, often dra-
matically so. To recognize it is the first step to coping

with it. Given half a chance, your true self will come back to inhabit its former place.

Wibberley liked to summarize his life as a "journey into confusion." In my opinion, that's what makes it all worthwhile. Total orderliness would soon bore *me* to death.

Leonard Wibberley died of a heart attack in Santa Monica, California, last November. In explaining his remarkable prolificacy, he said, "I couldn't reasonably recommend myself for employment to any company seriously in business, and so I had to write books."

POSTSCRIPT

I *really* believe in active older people. I count myself among them. I no longer want to spend months on location in Africa making a film. Nor, at this age, do I plan to raise the curtain at eight every evening for a long-run hit show. Those rigorous days were great but they *are* over.

Now that doesn't mean I want to stop communicating with my audience. As a performer, I have the unique opportunity to do what all older people should be able to do—present to the present what the past was and how we view the future. In primitive cultures in which the aged are revered, they function as the connecting link of experience.

When you reach my age, you've learned to sweep away the nonessentials and get to the point. It saves time—and time is precious now. I agree with Bernard Baruch that you can't retire experience. Older people do us an injustice if they choose not to share their experience. "To rest is to rust"; that's not my line, but it suits me. A woman named Thelma Ruble put it like this: "I'm not living on borrowed time. I'm living on given time."

Sometimes older people sound off about the good old days as though nothing today were worthwhile. Actually, those olden days were good mostly because we weren't—so old, or so good. Other oldsters fear ridicule and, therefore, they retreat. But, as James Thurber once said, "You might as well fall flat on your face as lean too far over backwards."

As we slide into the third stage of life we usually become more defined, freer, less serious. There are now more than fifty million of us who must make a statement for living fully, *within* the society, not on a siding.